Emile,

   Thank you for tutoring me
all these years. You are
the best stockpicker I know.
Reach for the stars,
settle for a million bucks!

copy #4

THE SCHOOL OF
HARD STOCKS

How to Get Your Portfolio Back to Even

DAVID E. SHAREK

First Edition

DavidSharek.com
14 Wall St., 20th Floor
New York, New York 10005

Library of Congress Cataloging-in-Publication Data

Sharek, David E.

The school of hard stocks: How to get your portfolio back to even/ by David E. Sharek.—1st ed.

Excludes index.

ISBN 978-0-615-22494-7

1. Investments. 2. Stocks. I Title.

Information in this book has been obtained from sources believed to be reliable. Neither DavidSharek.com (Shareks, LLC) nor LightningSource guarantees the accuracy or completeness of any information contained within this book. Neither David Sharek nor Shareks, LLC shall be responsible for any errors, omissions, or damages from use of this information. The information contained in this book is for historical purposes, and is not an attempt to provide investment advice. Past performance is no indication of future results. Investors should seek out professional investment advice before buying or selling any stock.

ISBN-10:   0-615-22494-6
ISBN-13: 978-0-615-22494-7

The last four years she has devoted her life to realizing my dream,
sacrificing her own career and goals to be my sidekick,
and molded me into the man I am today.

We traveled this journey together.

Without a doubt, Denise (my P.I.C.)
this book, my life, is devoted to you.

Special thanks goes to my clients,
who each have their own P.I.C.,
stuck with me through thick and thin
and always believed.

I wouldn't be where I am today
if it wasn't for those who
touched me
believed in me
gave everything to me (literally)
lived through my mistakes
and learning experiences
and thus allowed me to make it happen.

Thank you. I would not be where I am today if it were not for you.

You will always have a special place in my heart.

Contents

How to Build a Portfolio

What to Buy

When to Buy

How to Manage a Portfolio

When to Sell

Chapter A
How to Get Your Portfolio Back to Even

January 2, 2004

In the late 1990s, it seemed everyone was making money hand-over-fist in the stock market. Everyone but me, that is.

After graduating from SUNY Buffalo in February 1995, I packed my bags and headed south to Memphis, Tennessee. Born and raised in Buffalo, I needed a change. The long winters and poor economy brought my spirits down. I was convinced I could find a better life in the south.

Through college, I had supported myself by working as a salesman at a furniture store; so soon after arriving in Memphis, I got another job selling furniture. This new job had more earning potential, since it was a higher volume store. I focused on making the most money I could, worked long hours, and bumped my income from the $30,000-$35,000 range to the $60,000-$90,000 range. Living in a modest apartment with no dependents, and driving a Ford Ranger, I was cash-flowing enough to put $20,000-$30,000 into investments a year.

After analyzing where to invest my new-found fortune (fortune for me, anyway), I chose to invest my extra money in stocks. I had a deep fascination with stocks. The more I learned about them, the more I craved. Soon, researching stocks was what I lived for. I loved the thrill and opportunity to make big money. My heart raced when I woke up on a day the market was open, like a kid on Christmas morning. Since I had little market knowledge, I relied on stockbrokers for guidance, and made a few picks on my own.

I was awful at stocks

Even though the market was shooting higher, I was floundering. Everyone I heard of was making 30% a year during the last half of the '90s, but I was losing tens of thousands of dollars at a time. It seemed like every time I bought a stock high, it would go lower. When I bought a stock low, it went even lower. I tried trading for short term gains, and I ended up with long term losses. When I held for the long haul, I was stuck in dog stocks that continued to go down when the rest of the market went up. Penny stocks? Lost my shirt in **Service Merchandise (SME).** I hopped on buyout rumors, recommendations I heard on CNBC, or even a tip from a co-worker who got a tip from her brother, who got the tip from another guy who knew what he was talking about.

I continued to lose money in the market. Mentally, my confidence was shaken, but I was determined to figure out what I was doing wrong. It was as though I was always a step behind. I was the guy that the "Smart Money" sold to when it was time to get out.

Despite my severe losses, I knew in my heart I could turn things around and become a successful stock picker. I just needed to get better -- much better. To improve my investing skills, I read every piece of investing material I could. I subscribed to lots of financial magazines and newspapers, read countless books on investing, and tried to weed out who-knew-what-was-really-going-on from who-thought-they-knew-what-was-going-on. I swallowed information like a sponge.

Trouble was, as weeks turned to months and the more I learned, the more dangerous I became — and the more losses I created. My research was backfiring. What I needed was a change in my thought process. I needed to be quicker — smarter.

And sure enough, I began to figure out there was a secret world in the stock market. This secret world is where people could know — really know — where a stock is headed. History repeats itself in the stock market, and if we can figure out what made the past winners propel themselves from the pack, we can use the same rules as clues to pick tomorrow's winners today.

By 1998, I was finally putting the pieces of the stock market game together, and it was all making sense. I still wasn't good yet, but when something went wrong, I knew why. I had noticed a trend the best stocks possessed, one characteristic they all had in common, which was rarely talked about. The revelation I saw was:

Stock growth follows profit growth

One constant I always found when I researched the previous year's stock market winners was that they almost always had profits up big that year. If I invested in companies that had rapidly growing profits, I would own stocks that would go up. Conversely, if I owned shares in companies that had profits slowing, or declining, I would own stocks that would go down. So, I should buy a stock when the company's profits are growing, and sell a stock when profits are falling.

In 1998, I used high profit growth to select a list of stocks I thought would lead the market and make me rich. Those stocks were **Cisco System (CSCO)**, **Lucent Technologies (LU)**, **Dell Computer (DELL)**, **America Online (AOL)** and **Yahoo! (YHOO)**.

But, instead of selling my stocks and investing my portfolio only in those names, I bought only two of the five, Dell and Cisco, and continued to have faith in the rest of my portfolio. Instead of concentrating on the stocks I knew were superior, I owned Service Merchandise, **Boeing (BA)**, Bay Networks, Hadco, Mercury Finance, Union Planters, Monsanto, **Finish Line (FINL)**, **Pier 1 Imports (PIR)**, Regal Cinemas, Oxford Health and General Acceptance Corporation.

Years later, I had more losses than gains, even as the DELL and CSCO investments went through the roof. After I passed on buying LU, AOL and YHOO, they went up two-fold, six-fold and ten-fold. A bigger financial mistake than not selling my losers was not buying the stocks I thought would be the leaders.

I missed buying AOL

One decision that still haunts me the most is not buying America Online in 1997, or not buying it again in 1998. During 1997-1999 every Internet stock was galloping higher. It was not unheard of for one to go from $10 to $200 in a matter of months. Most Internet companies were not making profits, so to me, the run up in these names seemed too speculative and too much of a gamble.

AOL, on the other hand, was making profits. It was the granddaddy of the Internet stocks, but it was not getting the respect it deserved. AOL was making money and growing profits, but the stock price wasn't keeping up with the other Internet stocks like Yahoo! and **Amazon.com (AMZN).**

I first passed on AOL in 1997 and watched it triple in six months. After the stock corrected during 1998, I planned to really buy the stock this time. I watched AOL go back and forth from $10 to $15, back down to $10, before rising to $15. (All stock prices used in this book are adjusted for stocks splits which occurred before 2006. In reality, AOL was going back and forth between $80 and $120 at the time). Seeing a trend, I placed an order to buy $8,000 of AOL, if the stock were to fall to $10 a share.

AOL then dropped from $15 to $11 a share. My broker called me and asked if it would be OK to purchase the stock at the market price, but I was stubborn, and held to my $10 offer. Just before touching my "buy" price, AOL stopped falling and turned back up. The stock broke past $15 and kept climbing. In seven months the stock would hit $87 a share. I missed out on one of the best opportunities I would ever have.

Although I was aware of the basics of "buy when profits are growing/sell when profits are falling," I was still not executing. I was talking the talk, but not walking the walk. I was letting my emotions make my investment decisions. To truly consider myself a success in the market, I had to break all my bad habits and start with a fresh slate.

When We Should Have Bought and Sold America Online (AOL)

Chart One is AOL's one-year chart stock price from October 1997 through September 1998 (all charts are adjusted for splits which occurred before 2006). Throughout this book, we have helpful one-year and ten-year charts. You can tell the difference by looking at the time frame just below the company name and stock symbol.

One-year charts show a company's quarterly profit growth for each of the past four quarters at the bottom (see box in Chart One). The best stocks have a profit growth greater than 20%, so that's what we look for. Growth below 15% is not good enough. It is seen as a sell signal.

The rapidly-growing profits at the bottom of Chart One signify that AOL was a leading stock. My first chance to buy was on the left of this chart, at $5. My second chance was on the right, when the stock fell from $15 to $11.

Chart Two is a view of AOL during the next 12 months. Had I bought the stock at $11, I would have turned an $8,900 investment into a high of $87,000 before AOL dropped by 50%. Instead, I sat on my hands and let the opportunity pass me by. I continued to like the stock until AOL, a 75% grower, announced its merger with Time Warner, which was expected to grow only 15% annually. AOL Time Warner would be hard-pressed to continue rapid growth.

In **Chart Three** we fast-forward to April 2002. AOL is now merged with Time Warner. During 2001 and 2002, AOL was one of the most widely owned stocks in America, but it was having trouble growing profits (the N/As at the bottom of Chart Three depict losses, and they are followed by a 22% drop in profits). Still, as the stock price fell, analysts would consistently tout AOL as a "buy" – odd considering the profit picture. An unbiased investor who tracked profit growth easily saw the stock was screaming "sell."

10

What to Buy

We should have bought AOL in 1997 and 1998 because profit growth was greater than 100%.

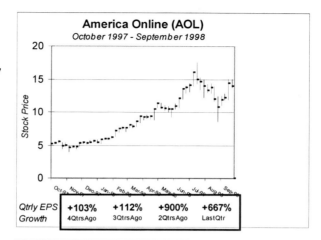

When to Buy

Here's the point when I should have bought. Notice the stock never hits the $10 price I was willing to pay, then races to $87.

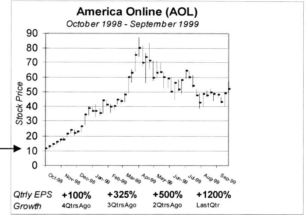

When to Sell

The sell signal was easy. In the bottom left corner the N/A means AOL Time Warner did not make a profit – the company lost money. Time to sell.

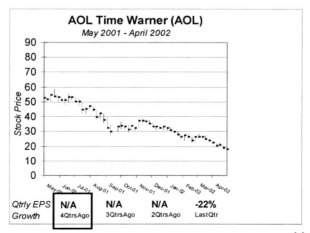

Get Your Portfolio Back to Even

This book focuses on getting portfolios back to even after the stock market crashed in March 2000. At the right is the S&P 500 from 1995-2005 – the period this book focuses on. History repeats itself in the stock market, so although this book explains a certain ten-year period, the concepts are timeless.

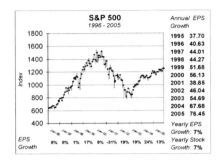

S&P 500 1996 - 2005	Annual EPS Growth
	1995 37.70
	1996 40.63
	1997 44.01
	1998 44.27
	1999 51.68
	2000 56.13
	2001 38.85
	2002 46.04
	2003 54.69
	2004 67.68
	2005 76.45

EPS Growth: 8% 8% 1% 17% 9% -31% 19% 19% 24% 13%

Yearly EPS Growth: 7%
Yearly Stock Growth: 7%

Above: Note the S&P 500 (1996-2006) almost got back to even. The stocks on the opposite page didn't.

I started to research stocks in 1996 and began to document my findings in November 2002 via the *Growth Stock Newsletter* and the *Commercial Appeal*, Memphis' predominate newspaper. The publication date is noted at the beginning of each chapter. Chapter Z in the A-Z guide was written in December 2005 and the book was assembled during 2006.

Growth Stocks were very good investments in the second-half of the 1990s, then got red-hot in 1999 and into first quarter of 2000. During the past five years (2001-2006), it was obvious that Intel, Microsoft, Cisco, Lucent and Time Warner were no longer growing profits as they had in the past. Still, many shareholders wouldn't sell their stocks – even after it was obvious the stocks weren't coming back.

Throughout this book, you will learn how to find the best stocks, but this knowledge is useless without positive action. Begin with a fresh start. It's not the stock you want to "get back to even," it's the money you care about. Disassociate yourself from bad stocks. Dump 'em, even if it means taking 99% losses. Not only does this new thinking include leaving the loser stocks you've been accustomed to, but we are going to dump the bad habits that got you there in the first place. A commitment to success is more important than knowing What to Buy, When to Buy, and When to Sell. Old winners seldom come back.

They Didn't Come Back

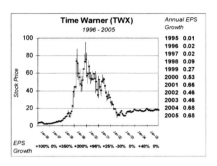

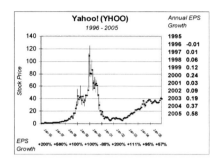

Above: AOL, now ***Time Warner (TWX)***, and YHOO were both big winners in the '90s. *Investors loaded up on the stocks at the end of their runs, and held far too long.*

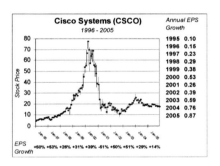

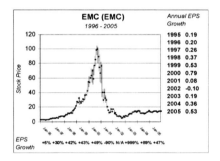

Above: *CSCO's profits fell in 2001, as did EMCs. Both well run companies were able to bring back profit growth, but their time had passed and neither stock bounced back.*

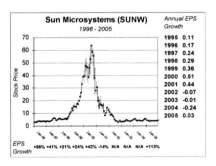

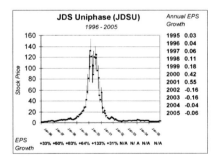

Above: *After the tech crash in 2000, SUNW and JDSU lost their ability to generate profits. Companies that lose money for longer than one year usually don't come back.*

13

Chapter B
How to Find the Best Stocks

September 10, 2004

I have always been intrigued by stocks that made the biggest gains, and I found it fascinating to study stocks that went up two, three, or four-fold in a single year. In my first four years as a stockbroker (1999-2002), I spent countless evenings researching the biggest winners of the past year, trying to spot trends or characteristics that the best stocks had. Many weekday evenings, I'd be the only person in the office burning the midnight oil, plotting charts, noting similarities, and searching for clues. On Saturday afternoons, I'd make a one-page synopsis of exactly what the super stock looked like before, during, and after its big run. I not only wanted to know what caused these stocks to take off to stratospheric heights, but how I could devise a way to find the future winners beforehand. I started uncovering secrets that only the smartest minds in the money management business knew; ones they shrewdly kept to themselves.

The Best Stocks Fit the Mold

Eventually, I was able to spot the pattern, or theme, that many superstar stocks possessed. From **Xerox (XRX)** during the 1960s to **Starbucks (SBUX)** during the 1990s, the great stocks had lots in common as they trounced the market. Time after time, each great stock had certain traits – appealing characteristics – that the other winners had. It was as if they were all poured from the same mold.

Armed with this knowledge, I found one stock after another that "fit the mold." Eventually, I built a portfolio compiled strictly with potential superstars.

After 2000, the stock market went from optimism to pessimism. Still, there was one constant. When the top mutual fund managers from the previous year were announced, each manager owned the same type of stocks – stocks I had been researching – stocks that "fit the mold."

Some of these stocks I owned in my managed portfolios. Some I merely tracked, because for one reason or another, I failed to buy them. Either way, we were on the same page. This gave me reason to believe that I was on the right track; the track leading to stock success.

Here are the characteristics that give investors the largest gains over extended periods of time. The traits of companies that fit the mold:

The Best Stocks are No-Brainers.

The best stocks are usually big gainers, year after year, for a long period of time; sometimes for decades. The **Home Depot's (HD)** and Dell's of the world were not flashes in the pan. They were consistent leaders year after year. Bet on a winner. You don't have to be a rocket scientist to find home runs. You don't have to be an analyst or have an MBA; you just need some common sense and a little basic math. Finding the best stocks is simpler than you think.

Another important stock tip is not to be afraid to buy a stock that is up for the year. Most people like to buy stocks when they are down, but good stocks go up and bad stocks go down. Usually, a good stock that is down is down for a reason, and that reason is that its time as a winner is up.

Buy Stocks with High Profit Growth

The first clue to search for when looking for great stocks is to consider companies with high profits growth – the higher the better. During a given year, most of the best stocks will have triple-digit profit growth. Since it's hard to keep doubling profits every year, the best stocks will grow at 35% or more, during a three-to-five year period. **Microsoft (MSFT)** grew profits 43% a year during the 1990s, but most people didn't pay attention to the stock until the middle of the decade.

Buy Stock with Catalysts

Catalysts often propel profits to new highs. A catalyst is a product or service that propels a company into profitability beyond their wildest dreams. Sales go through the roof. Profits grow even faster than sales, since demand is so strong the company can pretty much charge what they want. This is exactly what Microsoft did. It charged a premium price for their Windows software. When sales and profits started to slow, a new-and-improved Windows was introduced, and a fresh profit stream emerged. Remember Windows 95? Windows 98? Windows 2000? Those were catalysts.

The best stock gains will be derived from the power of compounding. There are two prerequisites to owning a stock that goes up ten-fold in ten-years. One is to hold the stock for ten-years.

Buy Stocks with Certainty

Stocks have personalities, just like people. Some you can trust, some you can't. When searching for winners, try to gauge whether the company will be able to make their estimated profits. Has their business been erratic historically, or are you fairly certain that the company will come through quarter after quarter? Is the stock in a stable industry like healthcare, or a wishy-washy sector with booming business one-year, but can't seem to make a profit in the following year? You worked too hard for your money; don't take chances with it. Own companies with high degrees of certainty.

During the 1990s, Microsoft had a high level of certainty, because it was the only big player in personal computer software. Whether people bought an **IBM (IBM)**, Dell or Compaq, it was MSFT that got the business. Its only competitor was **Apple (AAPL)**, which had its own operating system, but MFST easily squashed Apple's threat.

MSFT also had high certainty due to the PC revolution. With mainframes going out of style and personal computer sales dominating both the home and office, Microsoft had a steady stream of income each year.

Buy Stocks with Consistency

The best stocks grow profits consecutively every year. Each time annual profits are up, more investors should be hopping on the bandwagon. This is because the company is faithfully proving its success, year after year.

The cream-of-the-crop companies will grow in earnings each year and never incur a down year in profits. Notice in the table to the right that during the 1990s, Microsoft's EPS

Inside the Numbers: MSFT	EPS		P/E		Median Stock Price
1990	$0.03	x	28	=	$0.85
1991	0.05	x	33	=	1.67
1992	0.08	x	25	=	2.50
1993	0.10	x	26	=	2.62
1994	0.12	x	27	=	3.25
1995	0.15	x	35	=	5.23
1996	0.21	x	37	=	7.87
1997	0.33	x	42	=	14
1998	0.45	x	58	=	26
1999	0.70	x	67	=	47
2000	0.86	x	45	=	39

(earnings per share, the amount of profit per share of stock) went up every year, never down.

Buy Stocks with Growth Opportunity

When you're looking to add new stocks, first evaluate whether the company has ample room for growth. If their market is already saturated and its products have been around a while, like steel and automobiles, the company can't possibly keep growing at 30% a year. The PC revolution gave Microsoft lots of growth opportunity. With mainframes going out of style and personal computer sales dominating the market of both home and office, it was obvious that Microsoft was going to keep growing.

Microsoft (MSFT) Fit the Mold

Chart One is what Microsoft looked like in 1992, as a small, fast-growing software company. The first numbers I noticed were the outstanding quarterly profit growth figures for the previous four quarters, located at the bottom. It was clear to investors who followed profit growth at the time that MSFT was a leader. At the right are MSFT's profit figures since the company went public in 1986, with profits up every year. The P/E of 30 was low, considering that profits grew 47% last quarter. (Figures are adjusted for splits. MSFT was $73 at the time).

Chart Two is a ten-year chart of MSFT during the 1990s. Ten-year charts show annual profit growth rates along the bottom of the chart. If a company had been public for at least ten years, then we also calculate the rate at which profits compounded each year (*Yearly EPS Growth*) and the rate at which the stock compounded each year (*Yearly Stock Growth*).

In Microsoft's ten-year chart from the 90s, two characteristics stand out the most (besides the stock going wild). First, at the right, notice Microsoft's profits go up each year. Second, notice the high profit growth rates at the bottom of the chart. Compounding high rates of growth took profits from $0.03 to $0.70 in ten years, and fueled the stock's rise.

Chart Three is a one-year chart of MSFT just after the NASDAQ peaked in March 2000. When quarterly profits were slowing, money managers were selling, but many investors held on, thinking "it will be back". Notice quarterly profits at the bottom go from being up 23% to no-growth in four quarters. Microsoft stock, even after this decline, was still overvalued with a P/E of 31.

What to Buy

MSFT should have been bought in the early 90s, as profits were up each year, and the rate of quarterly profit growth was high.

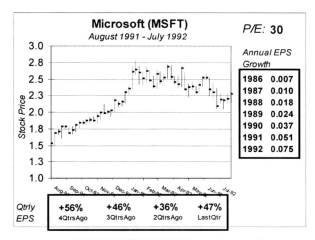

Microsoft (MSFT)	P/E: 30
August 1991 - July 1992	

Annual EPS Growth

Year	EPS
1986	0.007
1987	0.010
1988	0.018
1989	0.024
1990	0.037
1991	0.051
1992	0.075

Qtrly EPS	+56% 4QtrsAgo	+46% 3QtrsAgo	+36% 2QtrsAgo	+47% LastQtr

When to Hold

The best stocks are long-term winners. Hold stocks as long as profits continue to grow at 20% or more. Here, MSFT went from $0.61 to $58, almost one hundred fold.

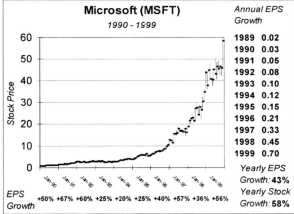

Microsoft (MSFT)
1990 - 1999

Annual EPS Growth

Year	EPS
1989	0.02
1990	0.03
1991	0.05
1992	0.08
1993	0.10
1994	0.12
1995	0.15
1996	0.21
1997	0.33
1998	0.45
1999	0.70

EPS Growth: +50% +67% +60% +25% +20% +25% +40% +57% +36% +56%

Yearly EPS Growth: 43%
Yearly Stock Growth: 58%

When to Sell

When Microsoft's profits slowed in 2000, it no longer fit the mold of a stock market leader. The 10% and 0% along the bottom were sell signals.

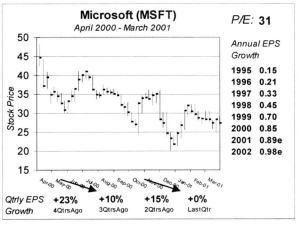

Microsoft (MSFT)	P/E: 31
April 2000 - March 2001	

Annual EPS Growth

Year	EPS
1995	0.15
1996	0.21
1997	0.33
1998	0.45
1999	0.70
2000	0.85
2001	0.89e
2002	0.98e

Qtrly EPS Growth	+23% 4QtrsAgo	+10% 3QtrsAgo	+15% 2QtrsAgo	+0% LastQtr

Buy Stocks in Hot Sectors

The main reason a stock goes up or down is that the stock market went up or down. The second leading factor behind a stock move is the sector, or industry, the stock is in. You could have the worst stock in your portfolio, but if the market is hot and the sector is favored, your stock could double or triple within a year. There have been lots of times I've owned a great stock, albeit in a bad sector, and watched the stock spiral downward. Trying to fight sector rotations is like attempting to paddle up a set of rapids.

When MSFT was knocking the lights out, all the tech stocks were in vogue. Software companies like **Peoplesoft (PSFT)**, **Adobe (ADBE)**, **Oracle (ORCL)**, and **Symantec (SYMC)**, which makes the Norton Anti-virus software, all went up more than ten-fold in price. Then, when the technology sector went down, all of these stocks fell. One key to winning in the market is to keep an eye on the sectors and have your money in the best ones.

Buy Stocks Below the Radar

Many people like to own what they know, but when it comes to making money in the stock market, it pays to find small and unknown stocks that nobody knows about. For a company to be able to grow profits at 35% a year for ten-years, it has to be small, since it is virtually impossible for large companies to accomplish such a feat. Imagine your current income growing at 35% a year for 10 years. That would be quite an accomplishment, and maybe hypothetical, depending on how much you're making. A teenager that mows lawns for extra money could accomplish the task, at least for a couple of years.

When you are in a stock before everyone else, you're in on the ground floor. Any new familiarity with the stock brings more prospective buyers. If more people want to buy the stock than sell the stock, the share price goes higher.

When I hear people telling me about a familiar stock such as Cisco, which was on everyone's radar in 2000, I know it's time to sell.

Buy Stocks that Beat the Street

One relatively unknown fact about the best stocks is that they beat earnings estimates while making their biggest runs. In other words, they underpromise and overdeliver.

In 1991, Microsoft was expected to grow next year's profits 26% and ended up with profit growth of 47% in 1992. MSFT nearly doubled during those two years.

In 1997, MSFT was expected to grow profits 18% and delighted investors with a 53% profit growth. Beating expectations helps to push the stock up 26% that year.

When companies start to miss expectations, start sniffing out new stock ideas. It may be time to part ways since missing expectations often signals a future decline in the stock price. In March 2000, during the NASDAQ's high, MSFT was expected to earn $0.95 in fiscal year 2001. Twelve months later, those expectations were lowered to $0.89, as the stock declined 50%.

High Profit Growth and a Low P/E Are a Powerful Combination

One important characteristic most investors miss is the combination of a rising P/E and growing profits. Together, these two can propel a stock price skyward. Notice in the Microsoft table earlier in this chapter (page 17) that MSFT had a P/E in the 20s during the early 1990s. As the decade progressed, the stock traded for a premium P/E of 67 in 1999. The combination of rapid profit growth and an expanding P/E created a powerful combination for Microsoft stock.

Chapter C
How to Calculate What a Stock is Worth

February 4, 2005

The key to managing your portfolio is to understand what each individual stock is truly worth. Once we find what we think the stock is worth, we can compare it to what the stock is now selling for. Then we can determine whether the stock should be higher, lower, or whether it is fairly valued. To understand how to value a stock, it's important to know how to value a small business.

We Start a Small Business

Let's pretend you and I purchase a hot dog stand, and call it Dave's Big Weenies. We each put $5,000, which amounts to $10,000 in total, into buying equipment. We won't run the operation; a manager will handle the day-to-day activities.

Under normal circumstances, businesses sell for "three to five times profits," which means three to five times the profit the company is making in a year. Normally, there are other factors involved in the business value, like equipment and inventory, but to keep things simple, we'll just look at profits.

Now, what's our business worth? To calculate this, we will multiply what the profits by the number of "years-worth-of-profits" someone will purchase the business for.

Year Three – What's the Business Worth?

We place our stand at a busy intersection and make $2,000 in profits in our first year, after all expenses. In the second year, business

Dave's Hot Dogs	Annual Profits	x	Years	=	Business Value
Year One	$2000				
Year Two	3000				
Year Three	5000	x	3	=	$15,000

grows, and we make an additional $3,000 in profits. In the third year, we make $5,000 more. Since you and I don't need the money, we put the $10,000 we made in the bank. In our eyes, the business is worth three-times profits of $5,000 a year, or $15,000.

Year Four – The Business Grows

In year four, we decide to expand operations and use the $10,000 in the bank to place an additional hot dog stand at another intersection. The second stand is also a

Dave's Hot Dogs	Annual Profits	x	Years	=	Business Value
Year One	$2000				
Year Two	3000				
Year Three	5000				
Year Four	10,000	x	3	=	$30,000

success and makes us $3,000 in profits. The original stand is now cranking, bringing in $7,000. At the end of year four, we are making $10,000 a year.

Year Five – Business is Booming

We are now entering year five. Since we made $10,000 last year, we take those profits and purchase our third stand. Our name continues to spread, and

Dave's Hot Dogs	Annual Profits	x	Years	=	Business Value
Year One	$2000				
Year Two	3000				
Year Three	5000				
Year Four	10,000				
Year Five	18,000	x	5	=	$90,000

all three stands prosper, as shown in the table. By the end of year five, the business is having its best year ever, bringing in $18,000 in profits. Our success is now obvious to anyone who has heard of Dave's Big Weenies. We think our business is now worth more than three-times profits, and it will take five years worth of profits to get us to sell.

The key point to take away from this example is that the business is worth more today than the $10,000 we put into it five-years ago, simply because it could not sell for less than it makes in profits in a year (duh).

How to Value a Business

As long as the external environment stays the same, that is if the government doesn't outlaw street vending, your original investment will grow under two conditions. First, profits continue to grow. Second, the number of "years-worth-of-profits" the company is worth stays the same or grows.

Also, the true worth of a business may not be the price that the market is willing to buy it for. When calculating a business value, we used one hard figure (profits) and one subjective figure (number of years). An emotional aspect is involved. The number of "years-worth-of-profits" could differ from person to person. It depends on how "hot" the business is at the time, or how people feel about future prospects. Additionally, notice the final price of $90,000 was triple of $30,000, which is what we thought the business was worth a year earlier.

Value a Stock Like a Business

Owning stocks is like owning a business, but instead of having partners, you have other shareholders. Within a publicly traded company, there are many more owners, each owning a portion of the company.

How to Value a Stock

This formula for valuing a stock is similar to the one used to value a small business. Multiply the profits a company is expected to make in the next year by the number of "years-worth-of-

How to Value a Stock	Profits	x	P/E	=	Stock
Year	Profits in earnings per share, or EPS	x	Years of profits the company is worth	=	What the stock is worth

profits," also known as the price/earning ratio, or P/E.

Finding the profits is easy. Earnings estimates for the year can be found online. You could do in-depth analysis to derive your own earnings estimates, but this is complex and time-consuming.

How to Figure a P/E

To figure a P/E, instead of using three or five as the "number-of-years" to multiply profits by, assume the P/E to be the rate profits are expected to grow at. Just drop the percentage mark. For example, companies that grow profits 25% annually are worth 25 times profits.

There are two ways to estimate how fast profits will grow. You can use the analysts' *Long Term Growth Rate* (LTG) estimate as the P/E. The LTG is the average of what each analyst who covers the stock thinks annual profit growth will be during the next five years. You can also calculate the P/E yourself. To find the annual growth rate, compare what the company should make this year to what it made last year. Take this number, drop the percentage mark, and use this figure as your P/E.

Publicly traded companies are considered to be longer-lasting than our little hot dog venture. We can assume that **Coca Cola (KO)** will be selling soft drinks longer than our stand will be serving hot dogs. Our firm may be able to last three to five years, but Coke should be making money ten to twenty years from now.

Don't use an unrealistic P/E

If a company is currently growing super fast, don't use an unrealistically high P/E. Companies sometimes grow 100% a year, but we can't assume the stock to be valued at a century's worth of profits. Also, a publicly traded company growing at 3% a year is probably worth more than three-times profits. So, try to assume a P/E of at least 10 for a stock in a mature industry like autos, a max of 40 to 45 for great stocks like MSFT during the 1990s, and 60 to 65 for superstars like AOL in the late 1990s.

How to Value a Stock – Hypothetical Example

Company A made $1.00 in profits last year, and is expected to make $1.20 this year. What is the company stock worth?

The profit part of the equation is given; the answer is $1.20. Calculate what you think the stock will be worth with this year's profits, not last year's. As with the hot dog stand, you don't want to sell yourself short by using last year's profits.

How many years worth of profits should the stock be selling for? Use the EPS x P/E = P to find the price. We have the EPS ($1.20) but now need the P/E. Figure a P/E by figuring the rate profits are growing, and drop the %. $(1.20 - 1.00)/1.00 =$ 20%. Drop the % and use 20 as your P/E.

Using our estimations, the stock is worth $24 a share.

How to Value a Stock	Profits	x	P/E	=	Stock Price
Last	1.00				
This	1.20	X	20	=	$24

The Story of Jos. A. Bank (JOSB)

Figuring what a stock is worth can lead to diamonds in the rough, if you come across an undervalued stock. In late 2001, I happened across **Jos. A. Bank (JOSB)**, an upscale men's clothing store that sells sweaters and suits. The stock had no analyst coverage at the time. Jos. A. Bank had a tough year in '01, partly due to the trend of casual work environments during the dot-com craze. But by the end of '01, it was clear that the dot-com thing wasn't working, and many dot-coms went bust. Ex-employees had to go get "real" jobs and wear suits again.

JOSB was below $4 a share, and profits were expected to be $0.60 the next year. It looked like the company was going to make more profits in the next four to five years than JOSB was worth. The market was terrible at the time; I found, or at least I thought I found, a diamond in the rough. I was so excited that I went office-to-office in the brokerage firm I was working at, jumping around like a kid with a new toy, telling everyone who would listen about what a Home Run this was going to be. But each time I told the story, I was the only one excited. Some brokers told me: "That's great!" But they didn't buy the stock. Two more concerned with finishing their personal conversation than talking stocks.

I was so convinced I had a big fish in JOSB that I sent my research to the head of equity research at the brokerage firm. A few days after sending my report, I called him to see what he thought. Instead of a pat on the back for a job well-done, the head of research told me he would forward my work to the retail analyst to see what he thought. A few weeks later, I got a nice letter from the head of research, saying he forwarded the analysis to the retail analyst, but that the firm had declined to pick up the coverage of JOSB. Instead, the analyst liked **Federated Department Stores (FD)**. Boring.

How to Value a Stock – Actual Example

What caught my interest with JOSB was the strong profit growth expected in 2002. We were at the end of 2001, and although profits were expected to grow in the single digits that year ($0.45 vs. $0.43), 2002's profits were expected to jump from $0.45 to $0.60. With a P/E of 6, I thought the stock should have been higher. What was JOSB worth?

The company was expected to make $0.60 over the next twelve months, so that's the profit part of the equation.

JOSB made $0.45 in profits during the last year, and over the next twelve months, it's expected to make $0.60. (0.60 – 0.45)/0.45 = 33%. Drop the % and use 33 as the P/E.

Inside the Numbers: JOSB	Profits	x	P/E	=	Stock Price
2001	0.45				
2002	0.60	X	33	=	$20

Using my estimates, JOSB was worth $20 a share. It was $4.

How Jos. A. Bank (JOSB) Became a Ten-Bagger

Chart One is JOSB in December of 2001. 2001's growth was slow, but 2002's profits looked to grow from $0.45 to $0.60, an estimated gain of 33%. Since the P/E was 6 this stock was a steal.

Chart Two is a view of Jos. A. Bank during 2002. The stock ran from $4 to $13, and then got cut in half. Volatile action is common within stocks that gain quickly in price. That's why you have to step back and assess the numbers unemotionally. After the pullback, JOSB was still selling only 8 times what it would earn that year.

Chart Three shows the stock from 1996 to 2005. Jos. A. Bank went up more than ten-fold (as Peter Lynch says "a ten-bagger") in four years. Profits grew an average of 44% a year, which proves that knowing how to value a stock can reap rich rewards.

The table to the right shows the stock's profits, P/E, and median price from 2001 to 2005. Profits expanded rapidly, and the P/E more than doubled. In the long run, the stock was an excellent investment. What amazed me even more than the fact that

Inside the Numbers: JOSB	EPS		P/E		Median Stock Price
2001	0.57	x	6	=	$3.5
2002	0.82	x	11	=	9
2003	1.17	x	16	=	19
2004	1.72	x	15	=	26
2005	2.45	x	16	=	39

analysts had not screamed "buy" was that another retailer didn't come in and buy the entire company. **Gap (GPS)** could have easily worked this into their lineup along with Old Navy or Banana Republic, especially when GPS was having trouble growing profits after the millennium. Gap could have easily bought the entire company, since Jos. A. Bank was worth less than $50 million.

What to Buy

Here is JOSB as of December 2001. Note profits were up 200% in the latest quarter. The stock never gets to $5, so a break over $5 would be the buy signal.

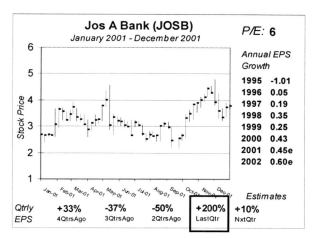

When to Buy

This is the next twelve months of JOSB. I bought JOSB in March 2002 at $5, after the stock broke out. I bought high, until the stock went higher.

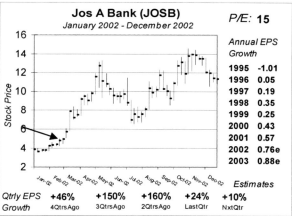

When to Hold

The breakout in Chart Two is pointed out in the bottom of the ten-year chart. During this decade, JOSB compounded at 45% a year.

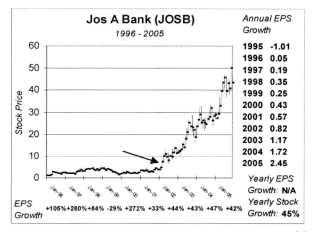

Chapter D
How to Grow Your Money Faster

June 3, 2005

The Rule of 72

The Rule of 72 is a mathematical equation which allows investors to calculate how long it will take to double your money, given a specified return. The formula states that you should take the number 72 and divide it by the return you expect, to figure out how many years it will take for your money to double.

Rule of 72	/	Rate of Return	=	Money Doubles in
72	/	3%	=	24 years
72	/	6%	=	12 years
72	/	8%	=	9 years
72	/	12%	=	6 years
72	/	16%	=	4.5 years
72	/	24%	=	3 years
72	/	36%	=	2 years

For example, if you settle for 3% CDs at the bank, the rule of thumb is that you will double your money in 24 years. Conversely, a mutual fund or a conservative stock might earn 12% a year, doubling your money in six years.

The Rule of 72 is not exact; it is merely a quick and simple way to estimate growth down the road. If you take a calculator to these figures, there will be some discrepancies.

After researching hundreds of stocks during the past decade, I have taken the Rule of 72 to another level—one which can be used to forecast what a stock could be worth in the future. It's my personal rule of 72:

Sharek's Rule of 72

The number of years it takes for a stock to double can be estimated by taking the number 72 and dividing by the expected profit growth rate (in EPS), provided

Sharek's Rule of 72	/	Companies Annual Profit	=	Stock Doubles in
72	/	12%	=	6 years
72	/	16%	=	4.5 years
72	/	24%	=	3 years
72	/	36%	=	2 years

that the stock's P/E stays consistent.

24% Growers Should Double Every Three Years

The company in the table to the right shows the reasoning behind Sharek's Rule of 72. Using the old Rule of 72, a 24% grower doubles profits every three years (72/24=3). Since the stock sold for 24 times earnings in the beginning of the run (fair value for a 24% grower) and 24 times

24% Grower Doubling Every Three Years	Profits	x	P/E	=	Stock Price
Start	$0.25	x	24	=	$6
Year 1					
Year 2					
Year 3	0.50	x	24	=	12
Year 4					
Year 5					
Year 6	1.00	x	24	=	24

at the end, the stock price quadrupled in six years.

The stock didn't necessarily have to go up exactly as much as the stock price. The stock could have earned a P/E higher or lower than what it started with, bringing the stock up or down accordingly.

The 24% grower in the previous table shows the reasoning behind my Rule of 72. The profit growth was used to determine the number of years it will take to double profits. Then I just used the same number (three years) to figure out how long it will take for the stock to double. This leads us to another fascinating discovery.

A Stock Should Rise or Fall at the Rate Company Profits Do

If the P/E were to remain the same at the beginning and the end of a run, a stock would rise or fall directly in proportion to what its profits are. In this case, since profits went up four-fold, the stock did too. So companies that grow profits 24% a year should have stocks that go up 24% a year, over an extended period of time (if the P/E is the same at the beginning and the end of the runs).

I use Sharek's Rule of 72 when I'm comparing the upside potential for one stock with another. **Proctor & Gamble (PG)** or **General Electric (GE)** may grow profits at 12% a year in the future, but that return pales in comparison to **Panera Bread (PNRA)**, which may grow profits at 24% annually. Of course, the risk in PG is less than that of PNRA, so to lower the risk, diversify into other fast-growing companies.

A main reason that people's portfolios "just sit there" is because the portfolios are littered with stocks that don't grow profits at a fast rate, if profits even grow at all. I can't stress enough that you must keep pushing forward into companies that are growing profits quickly, if you are determined to own the best stocks. Sell the slow growers and buy the fast growers, constantly.

36% Growers Should Double Every Two Years

One of the best ways to make big money in stocks is when you have even a little bit of money in a stock that grows profits at 36% a year — hypothetically doubling your money every two years. It's these Grand Slam Home Runs that we should be spending our time searching for. Ignore news articles about **Ford (F)**. Focus your time on searching for fast growing companies – you only have so much time during the day. These diamonds in the rough — the stocks that grow profits at 36% or more — can make a bad stock picker look like a genius.

Using Sharek's Rule of 72, a 36% grower would turn $10,000 into $320,000 in ten years (assuming the P/E is the same at the beginning and at the end). Sitting on some Blue Chip growing at 12% gets you to only $40,000.

$10,000 Compounded for Ten Years Using Different Rates of Return					
12% Grower		**24% Grower**		**36% Grower**	
Start	$10,000	Start	10,000	Start	10,000
6 yrs	20,000	3 yrs	20,000	2 yrs	20,000
12 yrs	40,000	6 yrs	40,000	4 yrs	40,000
		9 yrs	80,000	6 yrs	80,000
		12 yrs	160,000	8 yrs	160,000
				10 yrs	320,000
				12 yrs	640,000

I am convinced that searching for growth stocks is the best use of money an astute investor can make. The upside with the right growth stocks is so stupendous that even someone who only connects with a great stock once in a while can do extremely well, provided that they hang on to the supercharged stock.

But c'mon, having a stock go up thirty-two -fold? Can we really find companies capable of growing at 36% a year for a decade? Well, yes. Keep looking for companies growing profits at 36% presently. Maybe you will miss the first few years of growth, but keep in mind, companies come out with profit figures every three months, so that gives you four times a year to notice "XYZ Company announces a 36% jump in profits" in the news.

Why Chico's (CHS) Grew Money Faster

One superstar stock of 1996-2005 was **Chico's FAS (CHS)**, a clothing store for sophisticated women. Chico's is the prototype stock for explaining Sharek's Rule of 72, since profits compounded at more than 36% a year for ten years, giving Chico's investors the Home Run they were looking for.

Chart One is the one year chart of Chico's when I first researched the company in February 2001. I should have jumped all over Chico's, but unfortunately, I choked and didn't buy it. I didn't realize what a great stock it was. The best stocks are always flooded with high profits, and Chico's was all that. Instead, I bought **Christopher & Banks (CBK),** another women's retailer that fit the mold.

Chart Two shows what I was looking at when I finally bought Chico's in 2004. At the time, I thought there was no way the company could keep clicking on all cylinders like it had been, but I figured CHS could at least be counted on for 24% profit growth. That's a stock that could double in only three years, maybe quadruple in six. Chico's was also a leader in same-store sales at the time, a key positive for a specialty retail stock.

Chart Three is a ten-year chart of Chico's from June 1995 through May 2005. Profits go up each year, and the profit growth rate is healthy every year. The stock goes on a tear, giving Chico's investors 100 times their investment in only ten years.

Inside the Numbers: CHS	Profits	x	P/E	=	Stock Price
1995	$0.01	x	35	=	$0.35
1996	0.01	x	45	=	0.45
1997	0.02	x	15	=	0.30
1998	0.06	x	15	=	0.90
1999	0.10	x	17	=	1.75
2000	0.17	x	17	=	2.90
2001	0.25	x	19	=	4.65
2002	0.39	x	23	=	9
2003	0.57	x	25	=	14
2004	0.78	x	27	=	21
2005	1.06	x	32	=	34

What to Buy

Look at those quarterly profits across the bottom—smokin'. With a P/E of only 18, Chico's was a stock to buy. But of course, I didn't.

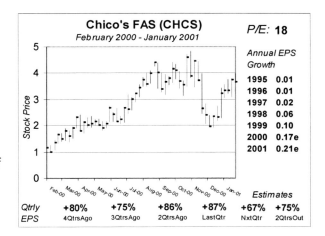

When to Buy

Here's when I bought CHS, after I watched the stock rise five-fold in three and a half years. Profit growth (bottom) was still exceptional.

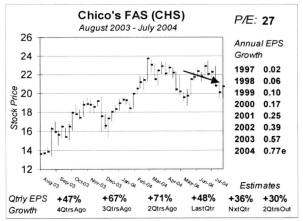

When to Hold

From August 1994 to July 2004, both Chico's stock price and profits grew at 41% a year, as stock growth matched profit growth.

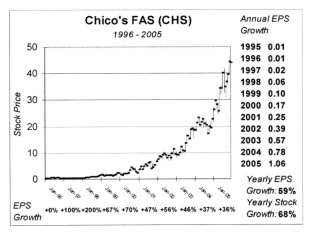

If You Are Undecided Between Two Stocks – Buy Them Both

I passed on the chance of buying Chico's after stumbling upon the stock in early 2001. Stuck in a bear market, I was looking for stocks that were strong enough to fight the tide. I was caught between buying Chico's and **Christopher & Banks (CBK)**. Both fit the mold of a winner, but I chose to buy only one (why, I don't know).

So I bought Christopher & Banks at $23 a share on Christmas Eve of 2001. Chico's went on to continue its torrid growth pace while Christopher & Banks went up to $29, fell all the way to $9, then worked back up to $19, where I threw in the towel and sold in February 2003.

Eighteen months later, I finally gave in and bought Chico's stock after it doubled – then doubled again – in four years, just as a 36% grower should, using Sharek's Rule of 72.

If you think you can pinpoint a stock that will go up one-hundred-fold, you're crazy. But big winners can be found by finding stocks that fit the mold, taking chances and buying ones which hold promise. And getting lucky. Very lucky.

The Affect of a Home Run on Your Portfolio

Let's look at the hypothetical performance of two portfolios. One has ten stocks that compound at 10% for ten years. The other portfolio has one stock that compounds at 35% and nine stocks that don't do anything – the stocks just sit there for ten years:

Portfolio One The Conservative Investor			Portfolio Two The Aggressive Investor		
Stock Investment Amount	Annual Growth Rate	Value After Ten Years	Stock Investment Amount	Annual Growth Rate	Value After Ten Years
$10,000	10%	23,579	$10,000	0%	10,000
10,000	10%	23,579	10,000	0%	10,000
10,000	10%	23,579	10,000	0%	10,000
10,000	10%	23,579	10,000	0%	10,000
10,000	10%	23,579	10,000	0%	10,000
10,000	10%	23,579	10,000	0%	10,000
10,000	10%	23,579	10,000	0%	10,000
10,000	10%	23,579	10,000	0%	10,000
10,000	10%	23,579	10,000	0%	10,000
10,000	10%	23,579	10,000	35%	148,937
Total Portfolio Value		**$235,790**	Total Portfolio Value		**$238,937**

Set Your Sights High by Looking For Companies That Can Grow Rapidly

This example also gives a ray of hope to investors who need some strong returns to "get their portfolios back to even." One reason I am constantly looking for fast-growing companies is if I can find two or three great stocks like the Home Run stock in Portfolio Two, all the work will be worthwhile.

The goal of managing your portfolio is to find a fast-growing company that can sustain the growth, hold it, and then find another. When I look back to 1990 and see companies with fast-growing profits like **Costco (COST)** and **International Game Technology (IGT)**, I wish I could go back and own these stocks before they made their big moves. In reality, I can't do that. What I can do is keep searching for tomorrow's stock market winners today.

Chapter E
Buy the No-Brainers

May 7, 2004

How could we have guessed ahead of time that the best stocks in recent decades would rise to such stratospheric heights? Were the investors, who bought these stocks on the rise, just plain lucky? No, it wasn't dumb luck that brought investors to Microsoft and Home Depot in the 1980s, and to Dell Computer in the 1990s. These stocks went up year after year after year. The best gains in the stock market are made in high-flying individual stocks that grow for a long, long time. These big winners are so easy to recognize, now that you have the tools necessary to spot the big winners. You should find that the best stocks are no-brainers.

The only thing you need is some common sense. Value the company as a business. Don't make emotional decisions to sell if your stock hits a certain price. Stick to the program and buy the best stocks – the ones that go up. As investors, we are in love with a deal. We love to pay less than what something is worth. This mentality leads us into stocks which aren't necessarily the best. Resist the temptation. Stick to the program. Bad stocks are down for a reason. Investors are so trained to think "buy low, sell high" that they consistently miss the easy winners.

The Best Stocks are No-Brainers

The best stocks to own are no-brainers. They scream for you to buy them. These stocks go up continuously. In our thought process, we must change our mentality to love stocks that are going up all the time and frown upon stocks that go down.

Don't be afraid of buying a stock that has made a huge run, because the Home Runs go up for a decade or longer. You might miss a year or two of the stock that is rising around 35% a year, like I did with Chico's, but you certainly have an opportunity to capture most of its gains. Even if you don't get a lion's share of the stock growth, you could still do better with a winner that has slowed down a bit, than you would with the dumpy stock that was beaten down.

When I look at the really big winners of the last three decades, they all had these qualities in common.

Three Characteristics of No-Brainer Stocks

1. For an extended number of years, the no-brainers showed profits growing at greater than 25% a year.

2. Profits were up each consecutive year with no up-years or down-years.

3. Buy the stock when its P/E is less than or equal to its profit growth rate.

That's it. That's the formula. You don't have to be super lucky or have a genius-level intelligence to hit home runs in the stock market. Of all the American companies to choose from, there are just a few that grow profits consecutively every year, so our search is quite narrow. When you know a certain stock has had a down year in profits, it can't be a no-brainer until it can deliver three consecutive years of record profits.

Wal-Mart was a No-Brainer

One of the best stocks of recent decades was **Wal-Mart (WMT).** In 1962, Sam L. Walton and his brother J. L. "Bud" Walton opened the first Wal-Mart store in Rogers, Arkansas. By 1967, WMT had grown to 24 stores with annual sales of $12.6 million. By 1970, it was a publicly traded company, offering 300,000 shares to the public at $16.50 per share. In 1973, Wal-Mart expanded to Tennessee.

In the early 1970s, shoppers clearly should have seen that the Wal-Mart concept was working: they would drive out of their way to shop at Wal-Mart. The company grew profits at 57% in 1971, then it backed up this growth with 49% growth in 1972 and 33% in 1973.

An accounting change resulted in only a slight increase in profits in 1974. By 1975, it was time for the Wal-Mart train to start rolling again.

1975 was the year to buy Wal-Mart

1975 was clearly the time to buy WMT, since profits that year would grow at an astounding rate of 67%. The company, opening in states one by one, had 125 stores in operation and went through its third two-for-one stock split. By this time, annual profit growth was averaging better than 40% a year.

Instead people stuck with Sears

I am shocked that investors in **Sears (S)** didn't see the light and dump their existing shares for Wal-Mart stock, considering the stores had a similar, although not identical, history. Richard Sears founded Sears in 1886, after receiving a set of watches he did not order. Instead of refusing the watches, he sold them himself on the railroad line (Sears worked in a railroad station and sold coal and lumber on the side.)

Sears started the R. W. Sears Company in Minneapolis, then moved the company to Chicago when he saw the trend of railroads, and hired Alvah C. Roebuck as a watchmaker. Rural stores in the 1890s were expensive places to shop, so Richard Sears used mail-order catalogs to show his merchandise and used the railroad to ship goods to people at prices much lower than local stores (sound familiar?). For example, a men's suit normally worth $3.50 cost $1.95, and a $50 bicycle was $15.50. He made up for low profit per item by looking for bargain merchandise he could sell in volume.

Sears even had a motto "Shop at Sears and Save." So when Wal-Mart became the king of low prices in the '70s, it was clear and obvious Wal-Mart was the next Sears. Sears shareholders probably spent their dividends at Wal-Mart.

In the table to the right, note WMT had a median P/E of 10 to 12 between 1975 and 1979. The P/E was less than the profit growth rate.

Even if you failed to buy Wal-Mart in the 1970s, you still had your chances in the 1980s. By early 1982, it was obvious that Wal-Mart was a leader for the ages. Its ten-year profit growth rate was 39%. Forbes ranked it the number-one general retailer for seven years straight. Even after missing a twenty-fold gain since 1975, new investors would still make 100 times their original investment, had they held on.

Inside the Numbers: WMT	Profits	X	P/E	=	Median Stock Price
1974	$0.002				
1975	0.003	x	12	=	$0.03
1976	0.004	x	12	=	0.05
1977	0.006	x	11	=	0.06
1978	0.008	x	12	=	0.09
1979	0.011	x	10	=	0.11
1980	0.014	x	12	=	0.17
1981	0.020	x	14	=	0.28
1982	0.029	x	20	=	0.57
1983	0.045	x	24	=	1.06
1984	0.06	x	20	=	1.20
1985	0.07	x	24	=	1.66
1986	0.10	x	26	=	2.59
1987	0.14	x	28	=	3.92
1988	0.19	x	19	=	3.63
1989	0.24	x	19	=	4.67
1990	0.29	x	25	=	7.11
1991	0.35	x	31	=	11
1992	0.44	x	34	=	15
1993	0.51	x	29	=	15
1994	0.59	x	22	=	13
1995	0.60	x	20	=	12
1996	0.67	x	18	=	12
1997	0.78	x	21	=	16
1998	0.99	x	30	=	30
1999	1.28	x	42	=	54
2000	1.40	x	39	=	55
2001	1.50	x	33	=	50
2002	1.81	x	30	=	54
2003	2.03	x	26	=	53
2004	2.41	x	23	=	56
2005	2.63	x	18	=	48
2006	2.92e	x	15	=	45

How Wal-Mart (WMT) Was a No-Brainer

Chart One shows Wal-Mart from 1975 to 1984, after accounting for all splits. Notice in 1975 profit growth goes from $0.002 to $0.003. That should have been our entry point, at 3 cents per share (it was $15 or so back then). That's it, you're in. Now just sit back and wait for profits to slow below 20%, which is your exit sign. Note the superior profit growth (bottom) year after year – WMT didn't hit the sell signal. This stock was a no-brainer.

Chart Two shows WMT's next ten years. If we missed buying WMT during the previous decade, we had an additional ten years to board this train. Here, Wal-Mart closely follows Sharek's Rule of 72, as the stock growth (25% a year) and profit growth (25% a year) are identical.

Long-term winners need more slack in terms of their profit growth. If you have good gains in the stock, and have held it three to five years, move the minimum profit growth to 15%. If you have owned the stock for a decade or more, change the sell signal to negative profit growth.

In Chart Two, profits are still growing strong, so WMT is still a buy at this point. The stock's performance during 1993-1994 shook out the weak investors who got scared when they focused on WMT's price decline.

Chart Three shows WMT from January 1995 to April 2004. From 1993-1996, the stock was flat, then went from $10 to $70. As Wal-Mart matured in the 1990s, profit growth slowed to the teens.

Notice on all three charts that profits never fell, and only slowed to single digit growth only twice. This means that long-term holders with large capital gains never encountered a sell signal.

Now, as of this writing in November 2006, this stock is basing again. Even though WMT stock has lagged during the past five years, the stock price has kept up with profit growth over the long-term.

When to Buy

The 1970s was a bad decade for stocks. WMT was a superior stock that bucked the downward trend. I always think of this chart when times get rough.

When to Hold

The market crashed in October 1987 and WMT fell almost 50%. The so-called "suckers" that got in at the high still made a ten-fold gain in the next 15 years, had they held.

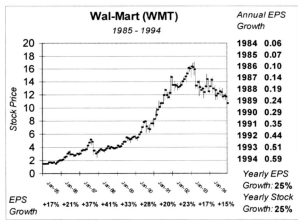

When to Hold

$1,000 invested in Wal-Mart in 1975, when profits were rising 67%, eventually would grow to $2,000,000 25 years later. Hold the no-brainers.

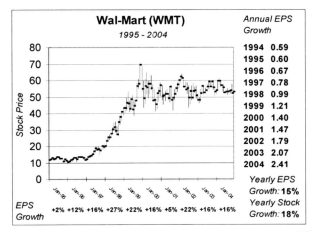

One lesson to learn from the WMT example is that the market really doesn't matter over the long term. Often I am asked, "What do you think the market is going to do?" To be frank, it really doesn't matter to me. All I need to do is seek out companies that grow profits year after year at high rates. Once I find one or two, I hold them and look for other prospective leaders, and I sell

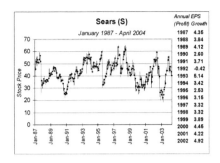

Above: Sears did nothing for 17 years. What did they do with all those profit? Spent them at Wal-Mart?

the underperforming stocks in the portfolio to fund these new purchases. As we saw Wal-Mart's Inside the Numbers table earlier in the chapter, profit growth unequivocally leads to stock growth.

If you own a no-brainer, don't get flustered when the market corrects. In the long term, the no-brainers will crush any market, a point I can't stress enough. The '70s was a terrible decade for stocks, but investors in the best stocks, the no-brainers, such as WMT, made money anyway.

The Best Stocks are the Most Volatile

The problem you will run into is that the best stocks are the most volatile during down markets. These stocks whip back and forth, and try to shake out the weak investors. Consequently, a portfolio filled with stock market leaders could go up more than the market as the market climbs, then fall more than the market during a correction.

The Two Types of Investors

I hold the firm belief that there are two types of investors:

1. Winners

Those who realize and accept what makes stocks go up or down.

2. Whiners

Those who are ignorant and refuse to see the light being shown to them.

All other investors are still undecided – in between – those who have yet to be taught, who still have a chance.

A minority of investors will be winners. These people have a self-realization that they are fully competent in managing the market (whether by themselves or having a winner manage their money for them). They have accepted the facts proven year after year, decade after decade, by winning and losing stocks.

Whiners blame others, complain about the market, then try to pull the winners over to the dark side by recommending the crap stocks that had led to their own demise.

Those who have not been shown what really makes a stock go up and down are on the fence. If shown the right way, these people have a chance at greatness. But even though many will be awarded such an opportunity, few will be able to recognize the evidence. Fortunately for us winners, the whiners give us someone to own the rest of the stocks and someone to dump our stocks on when it's time to sell.

Chapter F
Buy Stocks with High Profit Growth

April 4, 2003

If there is just one characteristic that separates the best stocks from the rest, it's high profit growth. To find the no-brainers at the beginning of their huge runs, search for companies growing profits rapidly. It's all about the profits. The best stocks grow profits faster and redeploy the excess cash to grow the business at a more rapid rate.

Follow the Leading Money Managers

Having a little success in 2002 after pledging myself to only buy — or even look at — stocks that fit the mold, I came across two articles in the July 29, 2002 edition of *Barron's*. The top money managers were profiled.

The first article, *Ruthian Record*, included an interview with Ira Unschuld of the Schroder Ultra Fund. The Schroder Ultra Fund had risen 1,587% cumulatively, since its inception in 1997 (about five years ago). The article listed some of the top holdings of the fund as of May 31, 2002 and December 31, 2001. The top holding of Unschuld's, **Hollywood Entertainment (HLYW)**, was also my top holding at the time. The other names were very familiar: ones I have researched in the past, stocks that fit the mold. I proceeded to research the other companies mentioned and noticed that the profit growth in each of those stocks was very high. The fund found its success — some of the best figures of all time — by owning stocks with high profit growth.

I read on. In the second article, *Barron's* ranked the top 100 fund managers. Leading the pack was Owen Thomas Barry, manager of the Bjurman Barry Micro-Cap Growth fund. The company's Web site cited five screens that were used for searching out new stocks. Number one: EPS Growth. The fund's top three holdings as of March 30, 2002 were:

Multimedia Gaming (MGAM) (which I owned), **Action Performance (ACTN)** (owned this one as well) and **Panera Bread (PNRA)** (one I should have owned). Clearly, I was on the right track.

Look at the Past to Foretell the Future

In *Wall Street 20th Century* by John Arthur Neumark, published in 1960, the story of Raytheon stock was told. The stock traveled "between 15 and 25" during 1955-1956, and "the conclusion was reached that a very substantial jump in earnings was in the making, and that missile activity itself was due for a tremendous rise." Then, "a severe setback in the stock market subsequently took place in the autumn of 1957, which carried the price down to a low of 17 ½. A careful re-evaluation suggested that this setback was purely temporary, and this subsequently proved to be the case. Beginning in October 1957 the stock rose almost without interruption until in April of 1959 a price of 74 was reached...in only three years earnings had jumped from the $0.23 ½ per share of 1956 to $3.08 per share in 1958."

In *Security Analysis*, Benjamin Graham and David Dodd wait until the third page in Chapter One to tell us that Wright Aeronautical made $1 a share in profits in 1922, when the stock was $8, then profits advanced to $3.77 in 1927, and leapt to $8 in 1928 as the stock hit $280.

To convince yourself that profit growth leads to stock growth, you have to look back at the Home Runs to see what they looked like before they made their moves. The stock market repeats itself, so tomorrow's stock market winners should somewhat resemble the winners of the past decades. When I looked back at some select stocks from the 1990s — some good, some great — to see what they had in common, this is what I found:

Look For a Catalyst

A new, unique, product often serves as a catalyst that spurs tremendous profitability within an organization. **Research in Motion's**

(RIMM) BlackBerry has been out for years, and it has really been a smash for company profits, since many businesses now have these phones for their top employees.

In addition to a new product launch, expanding an existing powerful brand or coming up with a unique service can produce incremental profit growth.

Catalysts from young companies are what we look for. Old, established companies have high cost structures, so a great new product might not double or triple profits.

It's All About the Profits

The two charts on the next page show 30 stocks of the 1990s. The left table lists some of the best stocks of the decade. The other stocks are on the right.

Notice how every single "great stock" had profit growth higher than every stock in the "good stocks" table. These two tables show irrefutable proof that all you have to do is look for the best profits each year to come up with at least some of the best stocks.

The very cream of the crop had the best profit growth within the group. Of those stocks, the one that stands out is **Dell Computer Corp. (DELL).**

Michael Dell started DELL in 1984 with only $1000, and founded it on the idea of building computers for customers and shipping them directly to them, eliminating the middleman. This direct shipment method allowed Dell to deliver similar goods for a much lower price. Consequently, sales and profits exploded.

Profit Growth Leads to Stock Growth

Great Stocks of the 1990s	Stock Growth	Profit Growth	Good Stocks of the 1990s	Stock Growth	Profit Growth
Amgen	51%	54%	Abbott Labs	16%	13%
Best Buy	59%	44%	Anheuser-Busch	14%	8%
Cardinal Health	24%	22%	Coca-Cola	20%	12%
Cisco Systems	94%	78%	Eastman Kodak	5%	12%
Dell	100%	45%	Emerson Electric	11%	9%
Harley-Davidson	39%	22%	Gillette	21%	11%
Home Depot	44%	30%	Johnson & Johnson	21%	14%
Intel	44%	33%	Kellogg	6%	6%
Medtronic	33%	22%	Kimberly-Clark	14%	8%
Microsoft	58%	43%	McDonald's	17%	11%
Oracle	48%	27%	Pepsico	13%	8%
Paychex	43%	29%	Philip Morris	5%	12%
Stryker	27%	23%	Proctor & Gamble	20%	11%
Sum Microsystems	54%	34%	Sears, Roebuck	-2%	-1%
Wal-Mart	32%	18%	Xerox	9%	6%
Great Stocks Average	**51%**	**35%**	**Good Stocks Average**	**13%**	**9%**

Dell (DELL) Had High Profit Growth

In **Chart One** we rewind to 1995. The loss in 1993 prevented DELL from fitting the mold until profits returned to record highs, which occurred here, giving us a fresh buy signal. Quarterly profit growth (bottom) was superb. After the back-and-forth move shown here, DELL broke out to an all-time high on Monday, April 17, 1995 at more than triple the volume traded than the previous Friday.

Chart Two is Dell during the decade of the 1990s. Notice the high rate at which profits grew during this time (except 1993). The loss posted in 1993 would have been a sell signal, but when profits rebounded the next year, it was time to get back in. Dell was clearly a great stock from 1995 to 1998 as profits grew 60%, 113%, 88% and 66% during that time.

Buying at the beginning of Chart Two would have yielded us a one-hundred-fold gain — assuming we held on and sold upon seeing the sell signals in Chart Three.

In **Chart Three** Dell's sell signals were easy to spot. Quarterly profit growth slowed to only 7% (in the bottom right corner), and the P/E was too high. I don't get scared by high P/E's, but I like to have explosive growth backing it up (as well as a history of beating the street). This peak you see in the right of the chart turned out to be the highest the stock would go on to hit (as of 2006).

Inside the Numbers: DELL	Profits		P/E		Median Stock Price
1990	$0.01	x	12	=	$0.12
1991	0.02	x	15	=	0.30
1992	0.04	x	13	=	0.52
1993	-0.02	x	N/A	=	0.49
1994	0.05	x	10	=	0.50
1995	0.09	x	8	=	0.78
1996	0.17	x	14	=	2.35
1997	0.32	x	25	=	8
1998	0.53	x	45	=	24
1999	0.68	x	63	=	43

When to Buy

A breakout occurs when a stock breaks through a price that has been a barrier in the past. The breakout point for DELL is here.

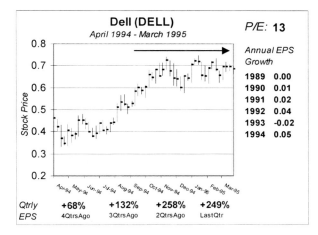

When to Hold

Once DELL broke out in 1995, annual profits (along the bottom) kept growing rapidly through 1999 – so this was a stock to hold, as a sell signal did not occur.

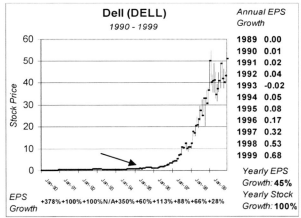

When to Sell

Note the 7% profit growth in the bottom right corner – this is a sell signal. DELL's P/E of 76 was very high, and is a second sell signal.

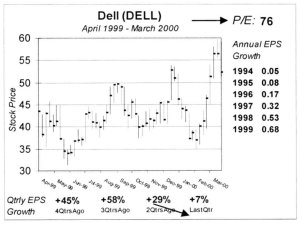

Dell was a difficult stock to read

In retrospect, although it seems Dell was a no-brainer, 1989's profit decline (shown in Chart Two on the previous page) and the 1993 loss would raise concern about the company's ability to grow profits consistently. Profits in 1990-1992 were obviously increasing at breathtaking pace, but the down year (1993) would have knocked me off the stock.

When I looked back at Dell's annual reports, the 1993 loss was mainly due to inventory write downs. Further reading uncovers the fact that losses were only in the second quarter, with the other three quarters being profitable, so you could have held.

The Best Stocks Show the Best Profit Growth

On the opposite page are some of the top stocks from 1990-2005. Along with Dell, **Cisco (CSCO)** and **EMC (EMC)** were the true big winners of the '90s. Even after the market went into bear mode in 2000, there were still opportunities to profit in stocks. The profits were there, all we had to do is look for them.

High Profit Growth Sparked these Stocks Higher

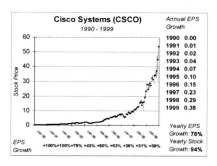

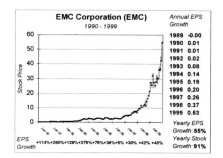

Above: Besides Dell, Cisco and EMC were the two best stocks to own in the Great Stocks of the 1990's table. These were two of the prettiest charts of the time.

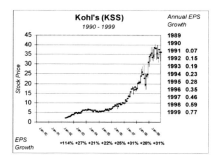

Above: Notice Kohl's profit growth during the 90s never fell below 20%.

Above: I messed up not buying PNRA In 2000, when profits hit a new high.

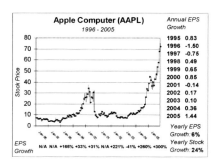

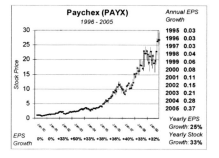

Above: Apple was a tough stock for me to read because profits were erratic.

Above: Thomas Golisano founded PAYX in 1971 with $3000 and one employee.

Chapter G
Buy Stocks with Consistency

June 6, 2003

Once you find a company growing profits rapidly, look to its profit history to find consistency, one of the easiest features that the best stocks display. Consistency is like Bigfoot's footprints in freshly fallen snow. Not only do they give you a clear picture, but a sense of where this thing might be headed.

When I speak of consistency, I mean consistently growing profits. Many big winners show profits up each year while they make their truly big moves. At the right are profits for Wal-Mart, Home Depot and Microsoft during the bull market from 1987 to 2000. I chose these three stocks because this was the period when they were considered the best stocks to own. Note each company grew profits each year during this period – never a down year. So, each and every year they all had record annual profits. Consistently growing profits without fail.

Consistent Profit Growth	Wal-Mart (WMT)	Microsoft (MSFT)	Home Depot (HD)
1987	.14	.01	.04
1988	.19	.01	.05
1989	.24	.02	.07
1990	.29	.02	.10
1991	.35	.04	.13
1992	.44	.06	.18
1993	.51	.09	.22
1994	.59	.12	.29
1995	.60	.16	.34
1996	.67	.18	.43
1997	.78	.28	.52
1998	.99	.41	.71
1999	1.28	.59	1.00
2000	1.40	.84	1.10

It's OK to invest in a stock that has profits fall for one or two years, as we saw with Dell earlier. But profits must return to record highs before the stock should be added to your portfolio. You can jump in early and buy if you think profits will be at all-time highs later that year.

Why Consistency is Important

Consistency is important because it shows what additional profits are doing to grow the company. For instance, if one hot dog stand made $10,000 a year, expanding to two stands should yield at least another dollar in profits. That comes to a total profit of $10,001 for the year, a record high. Anything less might mean the second location is losing money, or the first location is unable to repeat last year's success (with profits down).

One of the reasons people lose money in the stock market is by trusting, and investing in, companies that have not delivered consistency. If a company has a track record of up-and-down success, what makes you think anything will change in the future? Why gamble on a company with a history of being undependable, when you can go with proven winners?

Consistency Can Bail You Out

If a company keeps growing profits consistently, a losing position can eventually make it back to even. For instance, say you buy a stock for $20 a share that's making $1.00 in profits. Right after you purchase the stock, it drops to $15 a share. Now you're stuck.

If profits jump to $1.20 next year and $1.50 two years from now, it would be hard for the stock to stay down. Why? At $15, that $1.50 would be one-tenth of what the whole company is worth. Since profits are growing around 20% a year, the stock's really worth 20 times profits – or $30 a share. Even the worst bear market couldn't keep this stock down for long.

Stocks with high degrees of consistency are safer.

Why Stocks Went Down in 2000

To the right is a look at some of the biggest tech stocks/drug stocks in America during 2000-2002, with their profits from

Slowing Profits	Intel	AOL	EMC	Cisco	Bristol-Myers	Schering Plough
1999	1.17	0.27	0.54	0.36	1.87	1.42
2000	1.64	0.53	0.79	0.53	1.92	1.64
2001	0.52	0.46	0.09	0.41	1.04	1.58
2002	0.51	0.43	-0.05	0.39	1.05	1.42

the same period. Notice that the profits of these companies peaked in 2000. Not so coincidentally, their stock prices peaked around 2000 as well.

Since these are many of the largest companies in America, the lower stock prices brought the overall market down. Don't expect these names to lead the way anytime soon; they've got to get their consistency back, and this will take years. Personally, I probably won't consider a stock that has had a few down profit years until it comes back with a few straight years of record profits. There are too many other good companies to choose from.[1]

The 2000-2002 bear market creamed investors in stocks that did not possess consistent earnings. Meanwhile, companies that delivered consistency hit all-time highs.

Consecutive Record Quarters Provide Excellent Consistency

When I compare profits on a quarterly basis, I compare them to the same period a year ago. So the quarter ending December 31, 2005 would be compared to the December 31, 2004 quarter. Stocks that can

---

[1] I wrote this paragraph in June, 2003's newsletter. 2004 and 2005 were years where many of the stocks mentioned in the table had their profits rebound. Then, in mid-2006—three years after it had been written—strength in these names reappeared. Although I saw it, I did not buy in, focusing instead on tomorrow's winners.

hit profit records consecutively — meaning each quarter is greater than the quarter three months ago — have the finest consistency. Some of the best stocks grow profits at record highs each quarter.

Retailers rarely grow consecutively, since it's tough to have the first quarter (usually Jan-Mar) beat the Holiday Season (Oct-Dec).

Companies that grow consecutively prove to be immune from seasonality and are not tied closely to the economy, making them safer investments. Usually, these firms get paid on a fee basis, every quarter.

J2 Global Communication (JCOM) has a software service which converts faxes into emails, and vice versa, for business and households that don't have fax machines. At the right are

Growing Profits Consecutively JCOM	1st Qtr	2nd Qtr	3rd Qtr	4th Qtr
2001	-0.06	0.00	0.01	0.03
2002	0.07	0.14	0.16	0.19
2003	0.21	0.24	0.28	0.32

JCOM's profits from 2001-2003. Not only was each quarter's profit higher than the year before period, but it's higher than the previous quarter as well. JCOM opened in 2002 at $2 and the stock reached $47 by October 2003.

Affiliated Computer Services (ACS)

One of the most consistent companies in the stock market (as well as one of my favorite stocks) is **Affiliated Computer Services (ACS).** ACS is not much of a computer company, even though it sounds like one, it's more of a service company. It helps corporations and governments with their information technology/human resources tasks. Some of their clients include local, state and federal governments and commercial businesses. Basically, if you want to focus attention on growing your hot dog stand business, and don't want to mess with all that back office or computer stuff, you would hire ACS to do it for you and pay them a fee.

From its IPO in 1994 through 2003 ACS never missed earnings (profit) estimates, never cut guidance, and once had a string of 34 straight quarters of double-digit (+10%) profit growth. At the right is a ten-year chart of ACS from 1996 to 2005.

Affiliated Computer Services (ACS) 1996 - 2005	Annual EPS Growth
	1995 0.34
	1996 0.41
	1997 0.53
	1998 0.65
	1999 0.83
	2000 1.03
	2001 1.23
	2002 1.76
	2003 2.20
	2004 2.61
	2005 3.13

EPS Growth: +21% +29% +23% +28% +24% +19% +43% +25% +19% +20%
Yearly EPS Growth: 25%
Yearly Stock Growth: 19%

Above: ACS rose during the 2000-2002 bear market because it has consistent profit growth.

I bought ACS in 2001 after the company gave earnings and revenue estimates a full four quarters in advance – at a time when nothing in the stock market was dependable. Management boldly predicted profit growth of 31%, 41%, 44%, and 48% for the next four quarters, while stating revenue would be up 36%, 50%, 50%, and 59% as well. I thought: "These people are either crazy or know exactly what they are doing".

Since ACS's revenue is fee-based, and all their deals with customers are contracts, they know how much they will make months in advance.

So I bought the stock, and twelve months later the company came through with those lofty expectations. I caught the sweet spot of the move higher in the chart above.

When I first heard the ACS story, I thought it was similar to **Automatic Data Processing (ADP).**

Inside the Numbers: ACS	Profits		P/E		Median Stock Price
1996	$0.41	x	29	=	$12
1997	0.53	x	23	=	12
1998	0.65	x	26	=	17
1999	0.83	x	25	=	21
2000	1.03	x	22	=	23
2001	1.23	x	33	=	40
2002	1.76	x	26	=	45
2003	2.20	x	22	=	48
2004	2.61	x	21	=	54
2005	3.13	x	17	=	53

ADP Had Outstanding Consistency

ADP was considered the epitome of consistency, producing a streak of 41 years of double-digit profit growth, which just ended with the recent recession in 2003. Here's Peter Lynch, former manager of the Fidelity Magellan fund, writing about ADP in 1989 in *One Up on Wall Street*:

> *"How about Automatic Data Processing, which processes nine million paychecks a week for 180,000 small and medium-sized companies? His has been one of the all-time great opportunities: The company went public in 1961 and has increased earnings every year without a lapse. The worst it ever did was to earn 11 percent more than the previous year, and that was during the 1982-1983 recession when many companies reported losses....Automatic Data Processing sounds like the sort of high-tech enterprise I try to avoid, but in reality it's not a computer company. It uses computers to process paychecks, and users of technology are the biggest beneficiaries of high-tech. As competition drives down the price of computers, a firm like Automatic Data can buy the cheaper equipment, so its costs are continually reduced. This only adds to profits.....Without fanfare, this mundane enterprise that became public at six cents a share (adjusted for splits) now sells for $40 – $600 bagger long term.....So often we struggle to pick a winning stock, when all the while a winning stock has been struggling to pick us."[2]*

ADP proceeded to gain another 1,400% from the time Lynch's book was written to its peak in 2000, before dropping 50% from the highs – bringing the total return to around 4,200 times the original investment.

Additionally, dividends would be around $81,000 this year (2006), with the stock worth around $4 million (had an investor put $1000 into ADP in its infancy and held it consistently).

---

[2] *From "One Up on Wall Street" by Peter Lynch, page 85. Simon and Schuster, 1989.*

Stryker (SYK) is a Model of Consistency

Stryker will be one of the first stocks I look to for safety when the market starts to fall, since I want stocks I can trust, ones that come through in tough times. **Chart One** is a one-year view of what SYK looked like at the end of 2000. The first positive I notice is the string of annual profit growth (right) — consistent. As ACS did in 2000, Stryker loses one-third of its value in 2000, just before taking over as a market leader. As good stocks drop, dumb investors sell their good stocks to smart investors.

In **Chart Two** we see Stryker during 2001. We are in the midst of a bear market, and although SYK does well for the year, notice the stock had many 15% swings during the year. What if you owned SYK during that time and your statement went down 15% in a month? Would you have sold this stock?

On September 10, 2001, the day before 9/11, Stryker closed at $51. After the 9/11 terrorist attacks, SYK fell to a low of $45, then rebounded, closing the month at $52. I knew from tracking Stryker since 2000, that it was dependable, so this drop after 9/11 was my opportunity to buy SYK. But I hesitated and didn't buy, then watched the stock quickly bounce back.

Chart Three is Stryker's ten year chart. I didn't know of the company's exceptional consistency until reading in Value Line in June 2003 that Stryker grew profits at least 20% in 25 out of the past 26 years.

Inside the Numbers: SYK	Profits		P/E		Median Stock Price
1996	$0.26	x	23	=	$6
1997	0.32	x	28	=	9
1998	0.38	x	29	=	11
1999	0.41	x	37	=	15
2000	0.55	x	38	=	21
2001	0.67	x	40	=	27
2002	0.88	x	32	=	28
2003	1.12	x	32	=	36
2004	1.43	x	36	=	49
2005	1.75	x	28	=	49

What to Buy

Stryker was a stock to buy during 2000 because quarterly profits (along the bottom) kept growing consistently as tech darlings had profits drop like a rock.

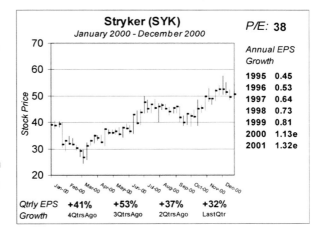

When to Buy

The time to buy SYK during 2001 was after 9/11 when the stock market reopened for trading – Stryker's consistency drove the stock back.

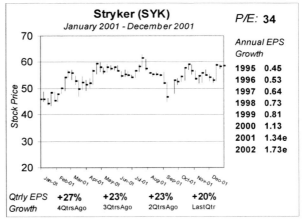

When to Hold

This is a ten-year view of Stryker from 1996 to 2005. Notice on the right that profits go up each year, showing amazing consistency.

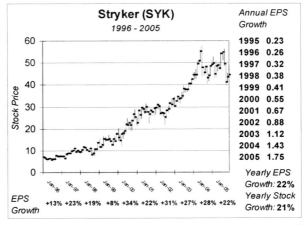

Chapter H
Buy Stocks with Certainty

May 2, 2003

"Stocks have personalities, just like people do"
-Emile Bizot III

Rolling in March 2000, I did thorough stock research that summer to confirm that I still owned the best stocks in the market. After exhaustive analysis, the companies that were growing profits best continued to be the leaders of 1999 — specifically tech stocks.

My research indicated that the chip stocks, networkers, and software companies were still the places to be. Profits were still growing faster than 50% in the stocks I loved, so the "correction" was for everybody else. I knew what I was doing.

Since I spent so long researching my stocks, and came up with such a brilliant display of long-term winners, I took my research to Emile Bizot III, a stockbroker in our brokerage firm who really knew stocks. Emile had grown a million-dollar business managing other people's money for 30 years. He made it through the 1970s, a time when the market went nowhere. The 1980s brought a bull market to stocks, and Emile was right in the thick of it, since his specialty was stocks.

Unlike most brokers, Emile realized that wealth was built in stocks, not mutual funds. He would ask me: "How many people do you know who got rich off mutual funds? How many by owning stocks?" Having his clients' assets in stocks meant he was in control, not some mutual fund manager whom he never met. The worst aspect of the brokerage business is losing other people's money. Emile was not going to put his future into the hands of someone unknown. He dealt with it himself.

Chapter H – Buy Stocks With Certainty

I was so excited when I dropped off my research binder for Emile to read. It was like I was the star student in school, handing in a research report to my professor, knowing I would get an A.

He returned my binder shortly after he read my research.

"So, what do you think?" I asked, looking for a pat on the back.

"It looks good on paper, but these companies won't earn what you think they will earn," he said.

I begged to differ, opening up the book to a chip stock, **PMC Sierra (PMCS),** which was growing profits in triple digits with a P/E of only 50. He said the company wouldn't hit those numbers. I said they would, since these were analyst figures. The analysts were the experts.

"No," he said. "Companies are like people. They, too, have personalities. Some you can trust, some you can't."

Emile pointed to the T.V. that was tuned into CNBC.

"You see that? Another earnings warning. These companies won't hit the numbers you are expecting," he said.

Whatever. I was the up-and-comer; he just didn't see the light. Fiber optics were the future, that was where the money would be made. I was following the rules of finding the best stocks, and since history repeats itself in the stock market, tech would bounce back.

In 2000, I had 80% or more of my assets in technology. Tech stocks tanked, and I got creamed in the tech stocks we owned. Most held up longer than others. **Seibel Systems (SEBL)** was one I owned which continued to hit new highs into November 2001.

But soon, all the tech stocks came crumbing down. The analysts were wrong. The companies didn't come through with profit growth like we expected. Many didn't come through with profits at all. **ADC Telecom**

(ADCT) continued to fall from $22 to $12, then I sold, before ADCT hit a low of $1.02. **Broadcom (BRCM)** and **Brocade (BRCD)** fell from over $100 to below $10 a share, and I sold along the way.

Applied Micro Circuits' (AMCC) CEO said business was great, couldn't be better, as the stock fell below $100 a share. No way could he have said that if it were not true. It was OK that he was dumping stock along the top; all these CEOs have to diversify. AMCC fell to $6 in Sep 2001, and I sold along the way down, again. Closer to the bottom than the top, again.

Emile was right. The companies didn't come through with the profits I expected. Not even close. By 2001, I cut my tech stock exposure to less than 20% of assets. But by then I had already lost around 45% after the NASDAQ crashed in March of 2000.

From that point forward, Emile was simply known as The Man.

The Man was now an icon – one who could read the market like a comic book, laughing at others along the way. The thought of putting people's money in stocks with high degrees of certainty was a concept that I was not aware of. Before, I always thought I would hit a Home Run and get myself out of any mess any time I fell behind.

Tough Markets Call For Certainty

Certainty is especially significant in tough market conditions, and here's why. The economy is usually slowing when we are in a bear market. So, those numbers you think will happen may not. Companies that have exposure to the economy, anything that could get cut if money is tight, are at great risk. Fortunately, stock market risk is greatly diffused by owning stocks that you are certain will hold their own.

One of the most important issues we face as investors is the ability to conserve capital in rough markets. When times are tough, don't take chances. It's better to opt for the sure thing than risk the principal of our portfolios. When times are tough, we need high degrees of certainty.

The thought of risking our hard-earned money makes most people cringe. Consequentially, they shun the stock market in fear of losing what little they have earned, an amount that may have taken a lifetime to accumulate. The problem is not the stock market; it's the stock selection.

Emile showed me how to invest in food stocks, because he said: "People gotta eat." He recommended investing in high-yielding stocks since people can at least make the dividends. Stay away from tech, The Man said, to which I defiantly replied: "All tech?"

"No tech. You can't trust 'em," he said.

Stocks with certainty are the ones in sectors that don't get pinched in recessions. Just think of your checkbook. What's a necessity and what's not? You have to eat, so food stocks and drug stores are safe havens. The electricity bill is the next priority, so utilities make good investments in tough markets. Next, your mortgage would be important, so Financials would be good investments. (Financials also benefit from lower interest rates given by the Federal Reserve in an effort to stimulate the economy.)

Our next priority would be to take care of our health. Drug companies, usually safe investments, were losing patents to generic drug makers. Consequently, generic drug stocks went higher and big drug stocks lost their certainty, since we could not depend on steady earnings growth. So I bought some generic drug stocks, and they went up.

Health insurance was a good investment due to the combination of certainty that people would pay for health insurance every month and the fact that premiums were rising. So I bought HMOs, too, and they went up as well.

UnitedHealth (UNH) Had Certainty

The chart to the right, **Chart One**, is a one-year view of **United Health (UNH)** as of February 2000, just before the market peaked one month later. This chart is a perfect example of what we should be looking for as the market changes direction. Notice the back-and-forth movement between $40 and $65. This stock gives us a buy signal if it breaks out past $8. Note quarterly profit growth is accelerating. Notice 2000 profit estimates (right) are $0.46 a share.

In **Chart Two**, one year later, UNH has broken out past $8 and doubled in price. With 2000 now in the books, the company actually made $0.53 a share (right side of chart), beating the street, and increasing the certainty factor. Also, a new breakout price of $16 is now established, a price that UnitedHealth would break through within months. After seeing the stock more than double, it was clear that a shift in market leadership to stocks with high certainty was happening.

Chart Three is UNH from 1996 to 2005. Ten-year charts help give me a big-picture view of what really went on with a stock. Notice UNH was neglected until the stock market topped in 2000. Then, the smart money went into stocks with high certainty. UnitedHealth certainly fit the bill of a safe stock, because they had just one down year in profits

Inside the Numbers: UNH	Profits		P/E		Median Stock Price
1996	$0.22	x	27	=	$6
1997	0.28	x	21	=	6
1998	0.33	x	18	=	6
1999	0.40	x	18	=	7
2000	0.53	x	21	=	11
2001	0.70	x	21	=	15
2002	1.06	x	20	=	21
2003	1.48	x	16	=	24
2004	1.97	x	18	=	36
2005	2.50	x	22	=	54

since 1988. It was beating the street, and most importantly, it was in a defensive healthcare sector. HMOs were having no trouble coming through as promised.

What to Buy

With a 31% profit growth in the latest quarter and a P/E of only 14, United Health was the stock to buy. The arrow shows when to buy – if UNH goes past $8.

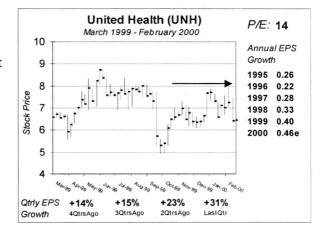

When to Buy

This is the following year for UNH. The stock broke out early, and set up another breakout point at $16. What a deal UNH was, growing at 32% with a 23 P/E.

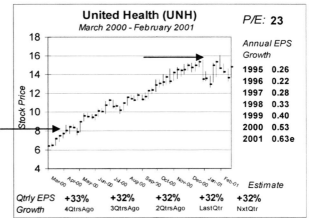

When to Hold

The arrows show the breakouts in Chart Two. UnitedHealth was a stock to hold through 2005 as profits grew faster than 20% each year.

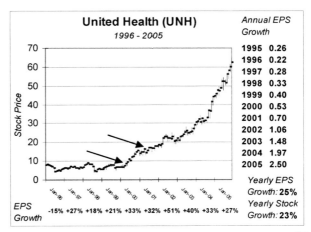

Not All Stocks Are Risky

Stocks are vastly different from each other. Some stocks you can trust immensely, some are completely undependable. The fact that risk varies from one stock to another is baffling for some investors, even after it is explained. An investor who has lost money in the market often believes that all stocks are risky, which is far from the truth. The problem isn't the stock market, it's the stock selection.

You Can Make Money in a Bear Market

Saying that you can't make money in bear markets is also hogwash. You can do well in bear markets if you invest where the big money is going – stocks with certainty. Billions of dollars are held in mutual funds, funds that are asked to invest in the market. As the managers shift money into certain stocks, you can ride the wave of inflows. Remember, fund managers don't want to blow people up. Like savvy stock buyers, they will invest in stocks with high levels of certainty when times are tough.

Certainty is something I now make sure I have in every stock I purchase. I want to know what the downside is. The way I look at it, if I just avoid the big mistakes, I'll make money.

The Effect of Certainty on a P/E

I believe that a company that informs us of its projections is more valuable than one that doesn't give analysts estimates. When a stock has higher certainty, I often think the P/E should be five higher than normal. For instance, if **General Electric (GE)** is expected to grow 11% a year, then I think the P/E should be 16, since GE has high certainty.

Six Stocks for a Bear Market

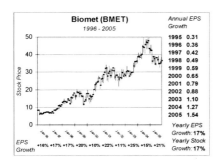

Above: *Biomet's profits have grown each year since at least 1988.*

Above: *For the faint at heart, there's Johnson & Johnson. 11% is not bad.*

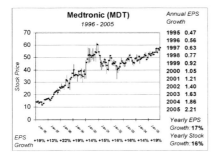

Above: *Medtronic is another medical device company.*

Above: *Paterson Companies is the top provider of dental equipment.*

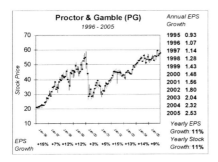

Above: *PG missed profit expectations in 2000 but bounced back as profits grew.*

Above: *In a bear market, you are still certain to pick up prescriptions.*

Chapter I
Buy Stocks with Growth Opportunity
November 5, 2004

Once the stock you research has passed the tests of consistency and certainty, look into the future and imagine how big the company will be years from now. Since we want our money to grow fast, we need to own stocks that grow rapidly. Common sense tells us that fast-growing stocks have companies behind them that are growing just as fast.

Can This Company Grow Rapidly For Ten Years?

Look for businesses with a potential market of millions of people. Try to imagine how much bigger a company could be in five, ten or twenty years. How many people bought an iPod but failed to see the huge number of iPods that would be sold by **Apple (AAPL)** worldwide?

If the company already has all its potential customers, then there's nowhere to grow. **Nokia's (NOK)** stock peaked in 2000 after everyone got a cell phone. This was a year before profits fell. If there's a dollar store on every corner, **Dollar Tree (DLTR)** and **99 Cents Only Stores (NDN)** don't have room to expand, so those are stocks we should avoid.

After 2001, it was obvious that **Cisco Systems (CSCO)** wouldn't be a leader for a long time. Cisco was a large company with little chance of growing as fast as it had in the previous decade. At most, Cisco could grow profits 15% a year.

Great Growth Stocks Have High P/Es

A high P/E ratio keeps many savvy investors from buying hot stocks.

A fast-growing company is worth a higher P/E than a slow grower because we want to own a little-piece of a small company that someday turns into a little-piece of a big company. Truly great stocks sometimes have P/Es two to five times larger than a mature company.

Some investors can't rationalize paying 50 times earnings for a company because they think that it means 50 years of profits. What we need to keep in mind is the growth rate of these high-flyers is so swift and strong, *the company is not selling for 50 times future profits – it's selling for 50 times present profits.* The fast grower with 50 P/E could make as much in profits during the next decade as the whole company is worth.

I Missed eBAY

I can tell you about growth opportunity because I have missed so many of the great ones. One of my recent mistakes was passing on **eBay (EBAY)** when it broke out at $17 in November 2002. I knew eBay was a great company and tracked the stock.

However, when I analyzed the stock, I saw that the P/E was too high, and passed on buying the stock. When I wrote of EBAY's greatness two years later, I should have tripled my money by then.

What went wrong? I have lots of excuses. I first thought the P/E was too high, but once the stock broke out and traded higher, I didn't want to buy it because the stock was "too high."

I really failed to see the growth opportunity aspect. I thought eBay was an auction site for used goods like antiques and baseball cards. Had I kicked the tires, checked out the site, and seen where the company would be years from now, I might have seen its vast potential to become bigger than Wal-Mart. Wal-Mart has to spend money on buildings, but eBay doesn't. Little did I know that cars would be auctioned off eBay, or that the company would be selling new goods — the same stuff available in stores — cheaper online since these little retailers selling the goods don't have high overhead.

eBay (EBAY) Had Growth Opportunity

Chart One is eBay as I saw it in November 2002. When eBay broke out at $17, I looked at the 2002 P/E of 80 (not shown) and I passed. Since it was November, 2003 was right around the corner. I should have looked ahead to next year. Since EBAY had growth opportunity, it was expected to make much more in 2003. Using 2003 estimates EBAY sold for 56 times profits – not bad considering profits grew 83% last quarter.

Chart Two shows the next 12 months of EBAY. The bull market started in March 2003 and EBAY was an early leader. Stocks that best fit the mold are usually the first to take off in an emerging bull market. If you sit on your hands, waiting for the confirmation that the bear has passed, you will miss a chunk of growth opportunity.

Chart Three shows the ten-year view of EBAY. Just think: this stock earned a penny in 1999 and four pennies in 2000 – at the time the P/E was off the charts. Profits exploded and so did the stock. The market saw what I didn't, and moved EBAY stock up before the profits materialized.

Now I realize the company was cheap when it broke out in November 2002, selling for only around 20 times what it went on to earn in 2005. Also, the breakout opportunity I missed at $17 in Chart One proved to be costly as the stock would go on to triple in three years.

Inside the Numbers: EBAY	Profits		P/E		Median Stock Price
1997	-	x	-	=	-
1998	$0.005	x	1400	=	$7
1999	0.01	x	1800	=	18
2000	0.04	x	475	=	19
2001	0.08	x	163	=	13
2002	0.21	x	71	=	15
2003	0.34	x	74	=	25
2004	0.57	x	79	=	45
2005	0.78	x	58	=	45

What to Buy

EBAY's profit growth of 83% in the latest quarter put EBAY on my watch list in 2002. EBAY was bumping its head on $16, so a move to $17 was my buy signal.

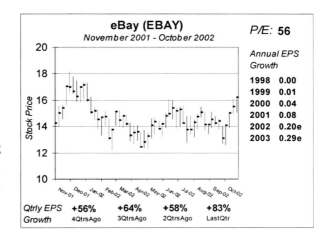

When to Buy

EBAY broke through $17 in November of 2002 and almost doubled the following year.

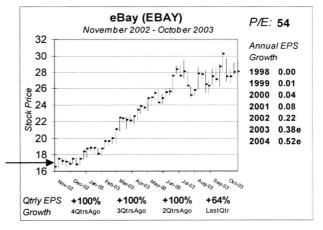

When to Hold

Investors who got hurt riding EBAY down in 2000 would get back to even again – and then some – as the profits bailed out the high P/E in the long run.

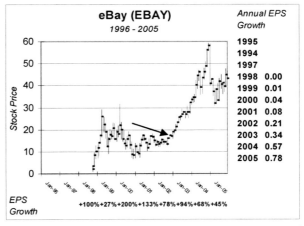

Ebay Led to Google

My mistake in missing EBAY helped me find another company with exceptional growth opportunity in October 2004. **Google (GOOG)** had tremendous growth opportunity because advertising dollars were leaking from traditional media (newspaper, television and radio) into new media (the Internet). Internet ads were deemed superior, since they targeted specific customers. But at the time, Internet advertising was only a small portion of total ad spending. Assume a company, having various advertising outlets, spent 2% of the entire ad budget on Google in 2004. An increase to 3% is a 50% revenue boost for Google. Also, no bricks and mortar meant much of sales flew straight to the bottom line — profits. To portray how the market saw GOOG during this time, I clipped an excerpt from my June 3, 2005 newsletter (GOOG was $288 the day before):

> *Our largest holding, Google (GOOG), is the hottest stock on the market. Here is a handful of reasons why the stock, in my opinion, will continue to move higher:*
>
> ***Google is still cheap.*** *I know the little guys are all saying "the stock is too high," but when valuing a stock, you need to look at the P/E, not the stock price. Which is better, having one $100 bill or ten $10 bills? They are both worth $100. So what's the difference in owning 100 shares of a $28 stock or 10 shares of a $280 one? When we value stocks, we look at the P/E; with a P/E of 53, this stock is not as expensive as* ***Yahoo (YHOO)*** *at 65 times earnings, and Google is a better company, looking at the numbers.*
>
> ***Google keeps beating the street.*** *We still don't have a handle on how much GOOG can make this year. Last October, the street was thinking GOOG could earn $2.82 in 2005. After beating the street, estimates got bumped to $3.67. Now, estimates stand at $5.17 with one quarter down and three to go.*

GOOG stock is under owned. When people on the street start telling me how great the stock is, that's when I know I should be looking to get out. But when I was calling clients to buy more Google last month, they really didn't want to do it. I had to tell the story to them all over again. Even the institutions have to do some catching-up. They, too, don't have as much Google as they need to; many have shunned the hottest stock on the market. Many mutual fund managers will rush to buy the stock as it keeps rising, just so they won't be embarrassed about not owning any GOOG at year end.

Google's figures are fantastic. We must keep in mind that this is a business we are buying into -- one which makes a ton of money. To the right is a table of Google's key financials. Most companies would be giddy about the annual growth that Google has had on a quarterly basis. Put another way, what if you were making $13,100 per quarter at your job in

Google's Profits and Sales		
Sep 02	$0.16	131,000,000
Dec 02	0.23	188,000,000
Mar 03	0.25	249,000,000
Jun 03	0.26	311,000,000
Sep 03	0.36	394,000,000
Dec 03	0.42	512,000,000
Mar 04	0.53	652,000,000
Jun 04	0.58	700,000,000
Sep 04	0.70	806,000,000
Dec 04	0.92	1,032,000,000
Mar 05	1.29	1,257,000,000

September 2002 (compared to Google's $131 million) and kept getting raises each quarter, reaching an astounding $125,700 last quarter (compared to Google's $1.25 billion)? Would your stock be going up in value?

Overhead is low. With no cost-of-good- sold and little labor, Google is pocketing a huge percentage of sales.

The online ad market is still small. Advertising dollars are still, for the most part, devoted to print, television and radio. The Internet allows companies to sell ads directly to people searching for their product.

Google Had Growth Opportunity

Chart One is Google when I bought it in October 2004. I wanted to get GOOG earlier, but had to wait until their first earnings report came out. Google executives did not give earnings guidance, and I saw that as a sign that they might not beat the street. When GOOG did beat the street, the stock ramped up rapidly, and I caught hold at $188.

Chart Two shows GOOG during the next 12 months. In February 2005, analysts estimated Google would make $5.07 in 2006, but I thought GOOG would make more like $6 a share. Sixty times earnings of $6 a share derived a $360 price target. When GOOG broke out at $220 I doubled my position. Google blew right past $360 price target on its way to $475.

In December 2005, I was thinking $1,000. Analysts estimated GOOG to earn $8.53 in 2006, but that was up from $7.32, $6.57 and $5.07. Ten bucks was a good guess. In 2005, the top Internet stocks were selling for 65 times earnings. I figured if Google made 10 bucks in 2006, then estimates for 2007 should be 40% higher — $14. A P/E of 65 x 14 = $910. Of course, the stock would then get hyped up, The "herd" would trample in and push the price to $1,000.

As **Chart Three** shows, Google digested its gains during 2006, and thus created a drag on my 2006 performance. 2006 was a frustrating year for me as a portfolio manager. I started out gaining 13% early on, then gave it all back. By mid-2006 I was even year-to-date, even though many of my other stocks were climbing. The reason I was spinning my wheels was because in 2005 Google was more than 10% of my assets under my management — before it doubled. So by the end of 2005, it accounted for more than 20% of clients' portfolios. Consequently, when GOOG went back-and-forth in 2006 many clients gave up altogether, and cashed in all the stocks in their portfolios (just as Google was poised to break out to all time highs).

What to Buy

One point not shown is Google was expected by many (including me) to make $4 in 2005, putting the P/E at a reasonable 48 — half the profit growth rate.

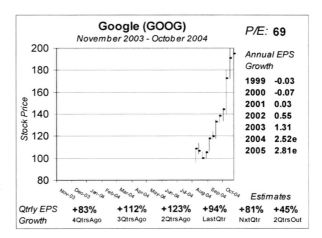

	Google (GOOG)	P/E: **69**
November 2003 - October 2004		

Annual EPS Growth

1999	-0.03
2000	-0.07
2001	0.03
2002	0.55
2003	1.31
2004	2.52e
2005	2.81e

Estimates

Qtrly EPS Growth	+83% 4QtrsAgo	+112% 3QtrsAgo	+123% 2QtrsAgo	+94% LastQtr	+81% NxtQtr	+45% 2QtrsOut

When to Buy

Google's breakout was here around $220 – this was the time to buy. Even after the stock almost doubled during that year, it was actually cheaper, since the P/E went down from 69 to 42.

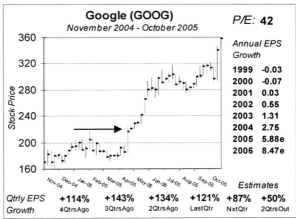

Google (GOOG)	P/E: **42**
November 2004 - October 2005	

Annual EPS Growth

1999	-0.03
2000	-0.07
2001	0.03
2002	0.55
2003	1.31
2004	2.75
2005	5.88e
2006	8.47e

Estimates

Qtrly EPS Growth	+114% 4QtrsAgo	+143% 3QtrsAgo	+134% 2QtrsAgo	+121% LastQtr	+87% NxtQtr	+50% 2QtrsOut

When to Hold

When Google was $200 a share, it was said to be expensive. Google had growth opportunity and the stock bolted higher.

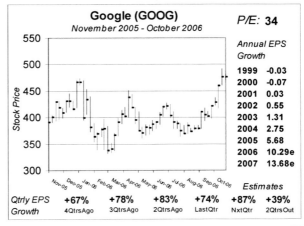

Google (GOOG)	P/E: **34**
November 2005 - October 2006	

Annual EPS Growth

1999	-0.03
2000	-0.07
2001	0.03
2002	0.55
2003	1.31
2004	2.75
2005	5.68
2006	10.29e
2007	13.68e

Estimates

Qtrly EPS Growth	+67% 4QtrsAgo	+78% 3QtrsAgo	+83% 2QtrsAgo	+74% LastQtr	+87% NxtQtr	+39% 2QtrsOut

Chapter J
Buy Stocks in Hot Sectors
February 4, 2004

Birds of a feather flock together, especially in the stock market. Stocks within an industry, or sector, usually move in tandem. In my opinion, the second biggest factor that determines the short-term movements of a stock is the sector or industry the stock is in. If your portfolio is overweight in the best sectors, it should outperform the market – whatever stocks you own. Conversely, if you get caught with stocks in the worst sectors, your portfolio can be dragged down even if you own great stocks.

Don't Paddle Upstream

The best metaphor that illustrates sector movements is rowing a boat in a river. Paddling up stream is exhausting, and you might not get anywhere. Sure, brag about being the strongest, but if the current is going against you, you're better off paddling downstream. Going downstream is fun; you can paddle if you want, but the current is gonna get you there anyway, so even a half-hearted effort will do. Sector moves are the same. If you get on the wrong side of the current, it's a tough way ahead.

I used to think I was smart enough to make money by picking great stocks in bad sectors, but I wasn't. When telecom leadership began to fade in 2000, specialty retailers, education stocks, homebuilders and gaming stocks took the reins. I was stubborn at first, but soon gave in and went with the current. Those investors who failed to adjust to the market suffered the worst losses from the bear market, whether they admitted it or not. On the other hand, those investors who lightened up on tech and overweighed the other sectors had their portfolios at all-time highs after the great market year of 2003.

How to Find the Best Sectors

In determining when to get into a sector, I put the most emphasis on searching for industries that have been out of favor for a while. It's better to get in early at the start of a long run and not be "late for the party." I then

Move In to a Sector When:
Many stocks have high profit growth.
Many stocks are breaking out in high volumes.
Sector has recently shown leadership.
The stocks are "beating the street."

look for multiple stocks that are breaking out within a sector and assess the earnings growth rates for those stocks to see if they have been beating the street.

It's really fun to cheat when you buy stocks in hot sectors – it's like taking an open book exam. If you see stocks in a sector breaking out,

look for other companies within the sector that have yet to breakout. As the stocks breakout, just hop on their coattails and ride the stocks higher. It's safer to invest this way, because the other stocks have paved the way — and if the other breakouts hold, there's a chance that yours will hold as well. The path has already been cleared.

Move Out of a Sector When:
Earnings start to slow.
Everybody's talking about it.
The run has lasted three years.
Stocks start selling off on high volume.
P/Es are high.
Companies are missing estimates.

Historically, drugs and medical, computer, communications technology, software, specialty retail, and leisure and entertainment groups have supplied more winners than most other groups.[3]

---

[3] *From 24 Essential Lessons for Investment Success by William J. O'Neil, McGraw Hill 2000, pg 36.*

There are quite a few clues to queue in to when trying to assess whether a sector is getting ready to turn down. Slow earnings and descending stock prices are two primary clues. The economy also plays a part in when to sell. If the economy goes into a recession, sectors with more certainty and consistency, like healthcare and food stocks, are the places to be.

When sectors turn down, profits we expect may not arrive. **Sun Microsystems' (SUNW)** and **Cisco (CSCO)** stocks both fell in late 2000 before their profits dropped in 2001. Computer hardware, computer software — anything having to do with electronics — was dangerous to invest in. The tech sector was down and out in 2001 and 2002.

The Next Tech Sector

When the bull market started in 2003, a new set of winners emerged, while many investors stuck with the tech darlings of the 1990s. IT outsourcing became the "next tech sector." IT outsourcing means having someone else do your information technology tasks for you. Overseas IT outsourcers have service centers located in Asian countries such as India and China. Because of lowered costs of living in those countries, salaries for software developers and engineers that would normally be $80,000 a year in the U.S. are $20,000 to $30,000 there. Customer service representatives are paid around $2 to $3 an hour, as opposed to $10 to $15 an hour in the States. Also, overseas outsourcing can avoid additional benefit costs such as health insurance and workers' compensation services, allowing American firms to increase profits without an additional up-tick in sales.

Spotting IT outsourcers as the next tech sector was easy, because the stocks within the sector had a history of consistent profit growth, year after year. People consider Dell, Intel, Microsoft, EMC, and Cisco to be the best tech stocks to own during the 1990s. During this time, only two of these companies had decreased profits, which lasted no more than a year. Otherwise, profit growth was consistent each year.

But when tech fell in 2000-2001, the IT outsourcers continued to grow profits, as shown in the table to the right. So when the

Consistent Profit Growth	Cognizant Tech. Solutions (CTSH)	Wipro LTD (WIT)	Satyam Computer (SAY)	Infosys Technologies (INFY)
1997				
1998	0.06			0.13
1999	0.10	0.06		0.25
2000	0.15	0.10		0.51
2001	0.19	0.13	0.24	0.63
2002	0.29	0.13	0.33	0.73

market took off in 2003, the money flowed into the stocks that continued to prosper in the toughest environment — the IT outsourcers.

In my opinion, the best stock to own this decade is **Cognizant Technology Solutions (CTSH)**. CTSH was originally an in-house technology department of Dun & Bradstreet, and it was spun off in 1998. The New Jersey-based company shows perfect consistency in their annual profits, which grew every year, even in the early 2000s when most other tech stocks suffered declining profits and layoffs, among other setbacks. Certainty is high with Cognizant Technology Solutions stock, because many IT deals are long term contracts. Customers often sign five-year contracts for services provided by Cognizant Technology Solutions, services that are similar to those provided by **Affiliate Computer Services (ACS)**. Growth opportunity is also strong, as companies outsource an increasing number of projects. Cell phone companies can outsource phone design and manufacturing, bringing new designs to the market in one-third of the time. But what really impresses me about CTSH is its profit growth rate. We all strive for that stock that can compound at a high rate for a long time. My personal goal is to own a stock that compounds at 36% a year for 10 years. According to Sharek's Rule of 72, that means turning $10,000 into $320,000. So far in this decade, CTSH is doing exactly that. If the sector stays hot, CTSH's success is likely to continue.

Cognizant Technology Solutions (CTSH)

These three charts show CTSH in 2003, 2004 and 2005.

The S&P 500, caught in a downward cycle since October 2000, broke out of its descending pattern in May 2003. When markets first turn up, the best stocks are the ones I look to buy, because they seem to rally first — and fast. **Chart One** shows CTSH, with profits up 50% in the previous quarter, breaking out in June 2003. With profits growing around 50% CTSH was one of the first stocks to break out in the new bull market.

Chart Two picks up where we left off in Chart One. After a spectacular 2003, a year when 35% portfolio gains were common, 2004 gave many investors a rate of return at around 10%. Old tech stocks like Microsoft, Cisco, and Oracle failed to return to prominence, while young guns like CTSH significantly outperformed. Note the tremendous profit growth CTSH displayed, both on an annual basis (right) and on a quarterly basis (bottom). With a P/E of 46, the stock was still not too high to buy.

Chart Three shows the beginning stages of what CTSH's ten-year chart might looks like at the end of 2009. Through 2005, profits continued to grow rapidly, but concern about industry growth slowing has held the shares back during the last year.

CTSH's earnings table at the right looks marvelous, with profits up big every year. Through 2005, Cognizant Technology Solutions looks like one of this decade's best stocks to own.

Inside the Numbers: CTSH	EPS		P/E		Median Stock Price
2000	$0.15	x	53	=	$8
2001	0.19	x	32	=	6
2002	0.29	x	31	=	9
2003	0.44	x	39	=	17
2004	0.70	x	44	=	31
2005	1.05	x	42	=	44

What to Buy

On the right, CTSH's *Annual EPS Growth* show profits up each year – this was what to buy. The arrow points to a breakout – this was When to Buy.

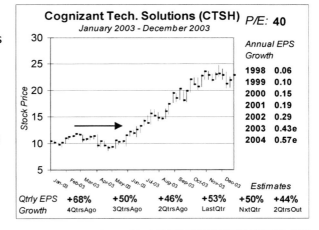

Cognizant Tech. Solutions (CTSH) P/E: **40**
January 2003 - December 2003

Annual EPS Growth

1998	0.06
1999	0.10
2000	0.15
2001	0.19
2002	0.29
2003	0.43e
2004	0.57e

Estimates

| Qtrly EPS Growth | +68% 4QtrsAgo | +50% 3QtrsAgo | +46% 2QtrsAgo | +53% LastQtr | +50% NxtQtr | +44% 2QtrsOut |

When to Buy

This stock gave us another breakout opportunity in September 2004, as quarterly profit growth (bottom) was greater than 50%.

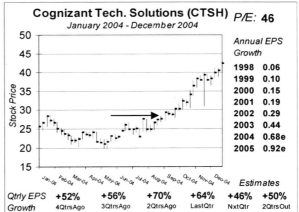

Cognizant Tech. Solutions (CTSH) P/E: **46**
January 2004 - December 2004

Annual EPS Growth

1998	0.06
1999	0.10
2000	0.15
2001	0.19
2002	0.29
2003	0.44
2004	0.68e
2005	0.92e

Estimates

| Qtrly EPS Growth | +52% 4QtrsAgo | +56% 3QtrsAgo | +70% 2QtrsAgo | +64% LastQtr | +46% NxtQtr | +50% 2QtrsOut |

When to Hold

The two breakouts are shown in this ten-year chart. From 2003 to 2005, CTSH quadrupled in price while Microsoft, Intel, Cisco and Oracle flat-lined as their sectors were weak.

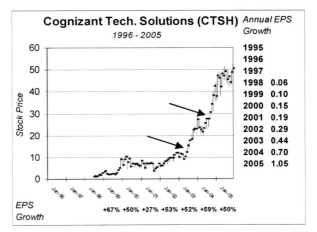

Cognizant Tech. Solutions (CTSH) Annual EPS Growth
1996 - 2005

1995	
1996	
1997	
1998	0.06
1999	0.10
2000	0.15
2001	0.19
2002	0.29
2003	0.44
2004	0.70
2005	1.05

EPS Growth   +67% +50% +27% +53% +52% +59% +50%

The Homebuilding Boom From 2000 to 2005

In 2000, after the tech stocks peaked, I looked for new hot sectors. At the time, homebuilders were broke out, one after another. The stocks were accumulated in high volume. Some days, it seemed the homebuilders were the only stocks going up.

Builders took off because interest rates were low, and because money flowed in from the stock market. Investors took big losses in the stock market during 2000-2002 and these people turned to real estate, which they thought "would never go down." This led to a speculative bubble in some U.S. markets such as Florida.

Since I wasn't familiar with the companies, and I couldn't tell the differences between them, I didn't get in early. I thought the best homebuilding stock was **Centex (CTX)** and tracked the stock, but didn't buy it until years later after most of the gains had been made.

During the first half of the decade, many investors thought the homebuilder stocks would crash just like the tech stocks did in 2000. But month after month, year after year, the homebuilders went higher. Finally, I threw in the towel and invested in a handful of names in 2003. I had written about how great the stocks were, but didn't eat my own cooking. I missed out on two doubles on each stock.

As 2004 and 2005 passed, interest rates stayed low, and this helped the builders. Speculation was high because people were buying second homes "as an investment" or "to flip." Soon, there were more homes than buyers.

Still, I'm here to tell you, the popular wisdom that "homebuilders would crash" was wrong. The nay-sayers missed one double, then a second, and a third. Many of these stocks went up ten-fold in price within five to ten years. Nobody really knew when the top would occur, or how many times the homebuilders would double by then.

One thing I distinctly recall is that the builders were strong, as they upped earnings estimates. When the stocks were beating the street and upping estimates, they were basing, breaking out, or heading higher. The top finally came when the company **Hovnanian (HOV)** lowered yearly earnings estimates. I bought HOV in October 2003 at $38 and sold in February 2006 at $46, and made 21%. The high was $73.

During the ensuing months, the whole sector went out of favor – even as the numbers continued to look good. Smart money was getting out as soon as HOV lowered guidance, because birds of a feather flock together. One by one I sold the builders until one remained in my portfolio: **D.R. Horton (DHI),** which looked to be the safest. I lost 19% on Centex and made 63% on **Beazer Homes (BZH)** after I sold both in May 2006. I continue to hold DHI, because the times you hear bad news about a sector are often times that its stocks turn up and go higher.

As the homebuilders peaked and fell, they only gave up half their value, a small price to pay for stocks that went up ten-fold. Stock selection within the sector didn't matter. It was a sector move: all the stocks in the sector went up or they all went down without discrepancy.

Same-Store Sales

Contrary to past decades, specialty retail has been a consistent leader since I started tracking the market. Specialty retailers are the companies that you would see in a mall or lined up in a shopping center. They often know their market well, and they've been beating the pants off the department stores through better product selection and merchandising.

One easy way to find a specialty retail leader is to look at the same-store sales figures. Buy the ones that have high same store sales. I have been amazed at the accuracy this one, simple number plays in finding the hot style of the season. From 2003 to 2004, **American Eagle Outfitters (AEOS)** tripled in price as its same-store sales were dressed to kill. **Children's Place (PLCE)**, **Starbucks (SBUX)** and **Chico's (CHS)** also flexed their same-store sales muscles in the early '00s.

Chapter K
Buy Stocks Below the Radar

October 3, 2003

When I started working in the investment business, my manager told me, "You can't beat the market." He said no matter how hard I tried, there was no way the little guy — or brokers, for that matter – could get better long-term returns than the market. We young stockbrokers were instructed to give up, and invest our clients' money in mutual funds and managed accounts.

I was told that there was no way I could make more for my clients than the large institutional money managers. The institutions spent millions of dollars on research. They sent people to travel the world, searching for clues, kicking the tires. With access to top-notch analysts, institutions would stay ahead of the curve and find that next big winner way before I could.

So I invested my clients' money with money managers and got burned. I placed my trust in other people to manage my clients' money. It was a disastrous mistake. One of my closest friends trusted me to invest his $150,000 nest egg. I, in turn, put my trust in money managers with excellent strategies and solid track records. The managers who preached growing profits proceeded to ride down the likes of **Sun Microsystems (SUNW)**, **Oracle (ORCL)**, and **WorldCom (WCOM),** well after profits fell (which was a sell signal). In a little more than a year, his IRA was reduced to $67,000.

Losing other people's money wasn't the only cause of distress; I also got blamed for something I didn't do. I didn't have control of the money, the money managers did; but I was the one that clients blamed for their losses. I left for work each day with a sinking feeling in my gut.

From then on, I decided to put all the research responsibilities on my shoulders.

As 2000 passed, I realized that Tech stocks weren't the "deals" they seemed to be. They had slowing profits and high P/Es, some at 50 or more. In January 2001, **Microsoft (MSFT)** delivered profit growth of 15%, but its P/E was a lofty 27. Too high. **Intel (INTC)** had us expecting a profit decrease of 7% that year. It had a P/E of 21, also too high. I searched and searched, but all the big companies I researched had poor prospects. **GE's (GE)** P/E was around 30, with profits expected to grow 15%. Too high, no upside. I would research all the household names to see if any fit the mold. Very few seemed attractive.

Scouring charts and research reports, I kept stumbling upon little companies that were growing like gangbusters. I found a smorgasbord of little diamonds in the rough: **AmeriCredit (ACF), Action Performance (ACTN), American Healthways (HWAY), Remington Oil (ROIL)** and **Hollywood Entertainment (HLYW).** They all had triple-digit profit growth and P/Es of around 10. Homebuilders looked tempting, too. **Lennar (LNR)** and **Beazer Homes (BZH)** both had profits up 88% in the first quarter of 2001, and sold for were only 9 times earnings.

Although I knew in my heart that these small stocks held the most promise, the analysts kept saying, "Buy the big companies." Why wasn't anyone talking up small stocks? *Because many of the great small caps did not have any analyst coverage at all.* Small caps were unknown creatures lurking below the radar of the big brokerage firms. Without a guiding voice to tell me what to do, I decided to be prudent and kept money in larger stocks. I was afraid to venture out on my own into uncharted waters. Taking a chance on placing client money in things they never heard of seemed risky.

Still, I knew something was going to give. Either the analysts had it right, that the old leaders would rise again, or there would be a changing of the guards—smaller, unknown names would bring the market back up.

The Market Shifted to Small Caps

By the end of 2001, a shift of power in the markets was apparent. Small caps were marching forward and the big tech stocks continued to decline, taking the NASDAQ with it. Most of the best small caps did not receive any headlines before running up, and were eventually noticed after they advanced in price (AmeriCredit got a lot of airtime after it made its move.) The stock I thought had the most to gain was **Alliance Gaming (ALLY)**. Alliance designed and manufactured slot machines for casinos under the name Bally's. The company formally changed its name to **Bally Technologies (BYI)** in 2006. Many people were familiar with Bally's slot machines in 2001, but the stock was obscure. Alliance Gaming was so small that no analysts covered it – it was below the radar of many investors, and it just needed a catalyst to get going.

I first noticed ALLY in January 2001, as it was trading just below $2.50 a share (it was actually below $10 before accounting for future splits). The company, which had been losing money for years, just turned the corner and was starting to make profits. (When the mutual fund companies look for stocks, they do computer searches to narrow down the list of prospective stocks to evaluate. These searches typically look for stocks that are selling for more than $10 to $12 per share. Consequently, ALLY was below the radar.)

What made Alliance Gaming a captivating story was that the company's management announced it was expecting to make $0.44 per share in earnings that year. Using my handy-dandy calculator, I was able to divide the $2.50 share price by $0.44 and came up with a P/E of only 5.5. Just guessing, I figured the P/E should have been 15 to 25, so the shares were meaningfully undervalued.

Since the company just started making steady profits, future profits would likely be triple-digit or more, since each quarter's profits would be compared against a year-ago loss. Also, the chart showed high buying volume, as ALLY rose from $1 to $2.50 during the past four months. Obviously, large institutions were accumulating shares.

Contrary to popular belief, brokerage firm analysts' recommendations don't push a stock up or down. Institutions — mutual funds and pensions — control the stock market. Little is spoken when institutions like a stock, but when a stock's trading volume and stock price are rising rapidly at the same time, you know big money is gobbling up shares; their footprints leave big impressions in the chart.

Though all my research pointed to ALLY going up, I didn't jump all over it. I didn't have my system down yet. I knew what to buy, but not when to buy (which was NOW). So I recommended the stock to clients, found a few who bought it, but most of them ended up with zero shares of ALLY. I was like a kid that showed everyone his ice cream, allowing it to melt on my sleeve.

The talk-the-talk but don't walk-the-walk was never more prevalent than on March 27, 2001. I was on a conference call with Louis Navellier, who founded Navellier and Associates, a money management firm managing $6 billion at the time. I was especially honored to be speaking to Mr. Navellier. He was the small cap king of the 1990s, gaining his investors an average annual return of 27% during the previous ten-year period, and wrote the top-returning stock newsletter during the past 15 years.

During the call, I asked for his opinion on the gaming sector (there were many stocks showing profit growth of 60% plus, with P/Es in the single digits). The one I specifically pointed out was Alliance Gaming. Mr. Navellier replied, "The gaming stocks are booming but our favorite play is **IGT (International Game Technology)**."

IGT (which I had followed, but did not own at the time) went on to have a good year, rising 42%. Alliance Gaming went on to become one of the top stocks of 2001, rising 569% in a bear market.

Alliance Gaming (AGI) Was Below the Radar

Chart One shows Alliance Gaming in early 2001, just after the company announced it would make $0.44 in profits for the year. Using simple math, I figured the stock was selling for less than 6 times earnings. I guessed the P/E should be 24 or so and the stock should go up four-fold just to be fairly valued. At the time, the gaming sector as a whole was hot, with many of the others in the industry sporting strong profit growth and low P/Es. Since this stock was never consistently profitable, the losses from earlier years were not seen as a negative in my eyes.

In **Chart Two** we pick up where we left off in Chart One. ALLY beat annual estimates and achieved the triple-digit profits I forecasted. Also, notice the strong correction from $10 to $5 after 9/11. Since Alliance Gaming was one of the strongest, fastest-growing companies, the stock incurred a steep correction when the market sold off, then quickly returned to new highs as soon as the market regained its balance.

Chart Three is the next 12 months of the stock. The sell signal was easy to see, and the stock gave investors lots of time to get out. My cost basis should now be $3 on a $15 stock. A five-fold move in a bear market would have alleviated a great deal of pressure. But I failed to act on an obvious winner, and didn't load up on the stock like I should have in Chart One.

The sell signal for ALLY came in April 2002, when we knew profits were expected to go down the next year. Overall, I should have had at least a quadruple. Instead, I found myself with merely a good story.

Inside the Numbers: ALLY	Profits		P/E		Median Stock Price
2000	$-0.29	x	N/A	=	$1.5
2001	0.57	x	13	=	7.5
2002	1.07	x	13	=	14

What to Buy

Alliance Gaming showed it was a stock to buy in early 2001, as quarterly profit growth was triple-digit and the stock's P/E was only 6.

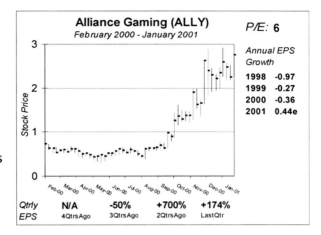

When to Buy

The following year gave us two buy signals as the stock broke out to new highs. Note the steep drop after 9/11, and the quick rebound.

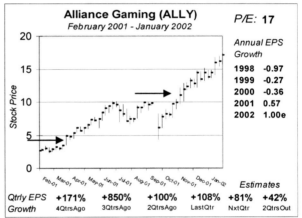

When to Sell

When profit growth slowed at the end of 2002, ALLY was no longer a leading stock, and should have been sold. Wish I owned it in the first place.

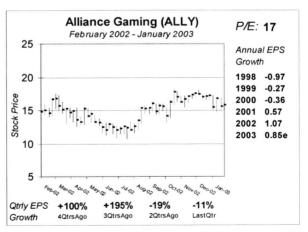

Molding a System of Success

As 2001 passed, I was having mixed success managing people's accounts. Some clients did well, others did not. I only had one client on my biggest winner, Alliance Gaming, but all my clients got hurt in Cisco Systems, which was my biggest holding as it crumbled from $80 to $22.

So I reviewed the stocks I was holding and realized even though I knew what the best stocks were, I often didn't own them. I was still hanging on to many stocks that did not fit the mold, even though I knew their time had passed.

I came to a conclusion: I needed to pretend I was starting off on a clean slate, that I didn't have an attachment to any stock. Then, I would ask myself, "Would I still buy this stock now?" If not, then I shouldn't own it in the first place.

In early 2002, I did an analysis to see what would have happened had I started 2001 in cash and bought only the stocks that fit the mold during the year. I went back through my notes, and plotted my buys and sells on a spreadsheet. To keep my emotions out of it, I allocated $1,000 to each purchase, and assumed I would sell if the stock dropped 10% from my purchase price, or if the stock no longer fit the mold. The hypothetical 2001 portfolio is on the next page.

After seeing how profitable 2001 could have been, I realize I needed to cut the fat from the portfolio and run with the winners.

The main thing I learned was to trust my own instincts beyond those of others. Stocks are just businesses, and I shouldn't care about what's going on with the market. There would always be investors who are willing to purchase profitable, growing businesses. Also, the old notions that "you can't beat the market" and "all stocks go down in a bear market" were clearly false, fabricated by those who weren't good enough to beat the market themselves.

Chapter K – Buy Stocks Below the Radar

Last but not least, I learned a great deal about the market's rotation. There is always a place to make money; we just need to find it. 2000 signaled a small cap rally which would extend more than five years. Early in the century, it was plain to see that the best stocks were traveling below the radar.

Hypothetical 2001								
Company	Symbol	Purchase Date	Sale Date	Purchase Price	Sale/Current Price	%Gain/ Loss	Investment	Current Value
TaroPharm	TARO	3/9/01		20	40	100%	1,000	2,000
Alliance Gaming	ALLY	3/23/01		6.9	29	320%	1,000	4,203
Americredit	ACF	4/12/01	9/21/01	15.2	13.68	-10%	1,000	900
Metro One	MTON	4/20/01		25	31	24%	1,000	1,240
Caremark	CMX	4/27/01	10/19/01	15.2	13.68	-10%	1,000	900
AmericanHealth	AMHC	5/4/01		13.5	32	137%	1,000	2,370
Ameripath	PATH	5/17/01		28.11	26.5	-6%	1,000	943
ActionPerform	ACTN	6/1/01		19	31	63%	1,000	1,632
AmeristarCasino	ASCA	6/1/01		12	25	108%	1,000	2,083
IntegraLifescien	IART	6/1/01		19	26	37%	1,000	1,368
ExpressScripts	ESRX	6/15/01	10/19/01	54	48.6	-10%	1,000	900
WashMutual	WM	6/22/01	10/17/01	37	33.3	-10%	1,000	900
PharmacRes	PRX	6/27/01		26.34	33	25%	1,000	1,253
FirstHorizPharm	FHRX	6/29/01		22	25.5	16%	1,000	1,159
Americredit	ACF	7/10/01	8/24/01	55.85	45	-19%	1,000	806
McKesson	MCK	7/23/01		37	37	0%	1,000	1,000
HealthSouth	HRC	8/1/01		17.9	15.22	-15%	1,000	850
Hollywood Ent	HLYW	8/7/01		9.9	14	41%	1,000	1,414
AffilCompServ	ACS	8/13/01		80.52	106	32%	1,000	1,316
AmerHomeMort	AMHC	9/20/01		19.88	17.9	-10%	1,000	900
CACI Inc	CACI	9/21/01		24	40	67%	1,000	1,667
Blockbuster	BBI	9/28/01		22	26	18%	1,000	1,182
Autozone	AZO	9/28/01		48	72	50%	1,000	1,500
AmerHealthway	AMHC	11/2/01		28	32	14%	1,000	1,143
ElectDataSyst	EDS	11/5/01		67	69	3%	1,000	1,030
AllianceGaming	ALLY	11/6/01		22.5	29	29%	1,000	1,289
TaroPharm	TARO	11/7/01		48	41.5	-14%	1,000	865
FTI Consulting	FCN	11/8/01		33	33	0%	1,000	1,000
Petsmart	PETM	11/8/01		8.42	9.7	15%	1,000	1,152
Nvidia	NVDA	11/12/01		51	67	31%	1,000	1,314
Lowes	LOW	11/13/01		40.5	47	16%	1,000	1,160
ActionPerform	ACTN	11/16/01		29	31	7%	1,000	1,069
United Health	UNH	11/20/01		70.5	72	2%	1,000	1,021
Best Buy	BBY	11/26/01		70	74	6%	1,000	1,057
O'Reilly Auto	ORLY	12/5/01		32.5	36	11%	1,000	1,108
MTR Gaming	MNTG	12/17/01		15	16	7%	1,000	1,067
Christ&Banks	CHBS	12/24/01		33.7	34	1%	1,000	1,009
Trades	37		**Current Positions 28**			29%	$37,000	$47,770
Losses Taken	9		Turnover ratio 24%					

Assuming Purchasing all stocks when "breaking out"
Selling after the stock drops 10%. ACF and TARO include higher losses, since they dropped dramatically before sale could have been made.
Holding each position for the "long Haul", not taking profits.
% Gain is average gain **per transaction.**
Not annualized (earlier purchases have had more time to appreciate).

Chapter L
Buy Stocks that Beat the Street

April 1, 2005

One of the best ways to search for the best stocks is to keep an eye out for companies that beat the street. For those of you not familiar with beat the street, "the Street" is short for street consensus, or the amount of profit the analysts who cover the stock thought the company would make, in a given quarter or year. "Beating the street" is when a company comes out with profits higher than analysts thought the company was going to make.

Companies that beat the street start a chain reaction which makes the company worth more than previously estimated — sometimes a lot more. In the example to the right, XYZ Corporation (XYZ) was looking to grow profits 20% in 2005, to $1.20 a share. Twenty percent growers are worth 20 times profits in my book, giving us a stock worth around $24.

XYZ Corp. Before Beating the Street	Profits		P/E		Stock Price
2004	1.00	x	20	=	$20
2005	1.20	x	20	=	24

But if the company were to start beating the $1.20 estimate, making us believe they were on their way to making $1.30 in profits this year, the stock would benefit in two ways. First the extra profits would grow the "Profits" used in figuring the fair value stock price. Second the P/E should be 30 instead of 20 since profits are now growing at 30%. The increase in both numbers used to figure what we think the stock is worth gives us a price target of $39 instead of the $24 we were thinking earlier.

XYZ Corp. After Beating the Street	Profits		P/E		Stock Price
2004	1.00	x	20	=	$20
2005	1.30	x	30	=	39

Chapter L – Buy Stocks that Beat the Street

Companies beat the street when they announce their quarterly earnings. ***Keeping a lookout for companies that beat the street and breakout on the same day lead you to finding the very best stocks in the market.*** After earnings are announced, it usually takes a few days after a company has beaten the street for the analysts to come up with new, often higher, profit projections. The more a company beats by, and the higher the estimates get upped, the better. Owning a company that just beat the street and guided higher is like owning a safer part of the market, because a company doesn't usually guide higher for the next quarter unless they really know they can hit it. On the other hand the biggest hits we often take in stocks are when companies miss the street, and the stock gets slammed.

Also, companies or analysts can up earnings estimates before earnings are announced if the business is trending well during the quarter. "Upping estimates" can also deliver a strong push for a stock. The best kind of upping estimates is when a company raises not only quarterly profit estimates, but annual profit estimates as well, showing the added success was not just a flash in the pan. To me, it doesn't matter when earnings get upped, it still counts as beating the street.

Another positive happens when a company beats the street repeatedly, quarter after quarter. This gives more security that we won't get hurt in this stock in the future since the biggest stock drops are often after a company misses earnings expectations. A more powerful combination is created when a stock that is growing earnings consecutively each quarter and beating the street every time they announce.

By keeping up with earnings estimates, you get a better feel for whether the company will up numbers during the quarter or beat the street at the end. You feel the pulse of the stock, and of a company's business. If a stock had been beating the street by a penny, but beats by a nickel in the latest quarter, it may be a signal business is accelerating, and we should buy more stock. I try to track all the top stocks that fit the mold, including ones I do not own, which gives me an understanding of the stock, and more certainty in names that consistently up estimates and beat the street.

UnitedHealth (UNH) was like a machine beating the street from March 2000 to December 2005. Here, UNH beats the street and each quarter's profits are larger than the previous quarter's. Obviously, management knew what they were doing, giving me confidence in UNH stock. UnitedHealth finally missed by a penny in the December of 2005, the same month the stock price peaked (as of November 2006).

Beware of cyclical industries, like microchips, steel and commodities. In these industries, a company can come out with good news and the stock can go down, sometimes unexplainably. This sell-off can be caused by the smart money seeing or hearing black clouds ahead, maybe in the company reports or on a conference call. Even though the numbers look great to you, and the company says business is booming, the stock may be bad news. I have ridden cyclical stocks down, only to find out the bad news for myself much after the fact.

UnitedHealth (UNH) Beating the Street		
Date	Estimate	Actual
Mar 2000	$0.11	0.12
Jun 2000	0.12	0.13
Sep 2000	0.13	0.14
Dec 2000	0.14	0.15
Mar 2001	0.15	0.18
Jun 2001	0.17	0.19
Sep 2001	0.18	0.20
Dec 2001	0.19	0.21
Mar 2002	0.22	0.23
Jun 2002	0.24	0.26
Sep 2002	0.26	0.28
Dec 2002	0.29	0.30
Mar 2003	0.31	0.33
Jun 2003	0.33	0.36
Sep 2003	0.37	0.39
Dec 2003	0.40	0.42
Mar 2004	0.43	0.44
Jun 2004	0.46	0.47
Sep 2004	0.50	0.52
Dec 2004	0.54	0.55
Mar 2005	0.57	0.58
Jun 2005	0.60	0.61
Sep 2005	0.63	0.64
Dec 2005	0.66	0.65

Source: Earnings.com

One of the great "beat the street" stocks from 2002 to 20005 was **Coach (COH)**. Coach makes upscale leather goods, primarily purses, wallets and handbags. Much of their business comes from Japan, where Coach products are a status symbol. Product quality is great, with the company giving a lifetime warranty on all its products.

Coach started making handbags in 1941, and was later acquired by Sara Lee in 1985. In 2000, Sara Lee distributed shares of COH to their shareholders.

Since its IPO in 2000, Coach has been one of the top stocks on the New York Stock Exchange. Propelling the stock price has been a consistent trend of the company beating the street and upping earnings estimates. To the right is a table illustrating the positive trend of COH upping yearly earnings estimates via press releases. Since stock growth follows profit growth, both Coach's earnings and COH stock rose about four-fold during this time.

Coach (COH) Upping Earnings Estimates			
Date	2003	2004	2005
Jul 2002	$0.29		
Sep 2002	0.30		
Oct 2002	0.32		
Jan 2003	0.35		
Feb 2003	0.37	0.42	
Apr 2003	0.39	0.45	
Jul 2003	0.40	0.48	
Oct 2003		0.55	
Jan 2004		0.60	
Apr 2004		0.66	0.78
Aug 2004		0.68	0.84
Sep 2004			0.86
Oct 2004			0.89
Jan 2005			0.94
Mar 2005			0.95

It is possible to look back at a company's history of beating the street, but I find it much better to track the changes in estimates as they happen. The computer won't show what the original estimates used to be. If we look at **Express Script's (ESRX)** 2005 fourth quarter on the computer, we will find they beat the street by 2 cents. Since I followed the stock, I noticed estimates were upped by $0.11 and $0.02 earlier, so ESRX really beat by $0.15.

Coach (COH) Beat the Street

Chart One is a view of Coach when I first started tracking the stock after they beat the street by $0.07 in early 2003. Below the quarterly profits are old quarterly estimates from my notes/research. For example, in the latest quarter COH was expected to have profits up 24% and beat the street with 39% profit growth.

Chart Two is the next 12 months of COH. Particularly impressive are the two middle quarters in the table. In these two quarters the company trounced previous estimates. Not-so-coincidentally the stock went from $12 to $20 during that time. I still didn't own COH at this point, even though in retrospect owning it was a no-brainer.

Chart Three is Coach through February 2005. In July 2004, I finally threw in the towel and bought COH at $21 a share, after the company beat the street by $0.02 and upped estimates by $0.01 earlier in the quarter. Through 2006, this has been a successful purchase, but after the company only beat by a penny in the December 2005 quarter, I noticed a trend that Coach had not been beating the street as handily as in the past.

The profit table to the right shows COH's median price went up almost ten fold from 2000 to 2005. Profits didn't grow quite so fast, the stock was helped out with a P/E ratio that expanded from 21 to 28.

Inside the Numbers: COH	EPS		P/E		Median Stock Price
2000	$0.14	x	21	=	$3
2001	0.20	x	20	=	4
2002	0.24	x	29	=	7
2003	0.40	x	35	=	14
2004	0.68	x	34	=	23
2005	1.00	x	28	=	28

What to Buy

We should have bought COH during 2002. Note the July '02 drop which flushed out many investors. That was a weird month that saw stocks drop around 10%.

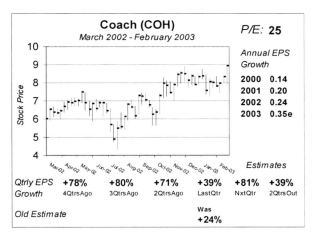

When to Buy

In Chart One we see COH couldn't get past $9. A move over $9 was When to Buy. In Chart Two COH breaks $9 in March of 2003 – during the first month of the new bull market.

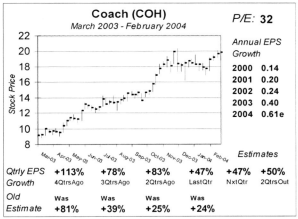

When to Hold

Coach continued higher the next twelve months, as quarterly profit growth continued to trounce previous profit estimates.

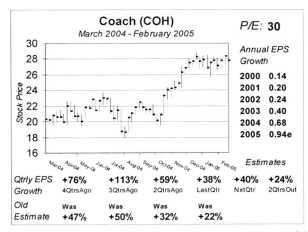

99

There are plenty examples of the best stocks beating the street. The figures on the next two pages are as happened. I didn't take stock splits into account as I did in the rest of the book because that woud take away from the aura surrounding the beating. A one cent beat (after splits) is not as sexy as beating the street by 8 cents.

- In 1997-2000 **Yahoo! (YHOO)** was thought to be an expensive stock, because it had a high P/E. But YHOO was always beating the street, so we didn't know how much Yahoo! was going to make in the future. To the right are YHOO's actual EPS and what the company beat the street by in each of the quarters mentioned. Beating the street had a profound effect on the YHOO stock during 1997-1999.

Yahoo! (YHOO) Beating the Street		
Quarter	EPS	Beat by
Dec 1996	0.00	5 cents
Mar 1997	0.01	1 cent
Jun 1997	0.02	3 cents
Sep 1997	0.03	2 cents
Dec 1997	0.05	2 cents
Mar 1998	0.08	4 cents
Jun 1998	0.15	6 cents
Sep 1998	0.15	6 cents
Dec 1998	0.21	5 cents
Mar 1999	0.11	3 cents
Jun 1999	0.11	3 cents
Sep 1999	0.14	5 cents
Dec 1999	0.19	4 cents

- In March of 1999, **Qualcomm (QCOM)** was supposed to make $1.38 for the year. Then after quarterly earnings were announced, one analyst upped his estimates to $1.96 a share. QCOM truly made $2.46 in 1999. 1999 was so good that during the year next year's (2000) estimates jumped from $1.38 to $2.73 to $3.90 – before the year 2000 ever came around – as QCOM rose 2587% in '99.

- **NutriSystem (NTRI)** went from $3 to $75 in 2005-2006,

NTRI Beating the Street	3/06	6/06 Est.	9/06 Est.	2006 Est.	2007 Est.
April 24, 2006	0.40e	0.35	0.35	1.38	1.92
April 25, 2006	0.60a	0.44	0.42	1.79	2.40

as it repeatedly crushed earnings estimates and guided higher. On Tuesday, April 25, 2006 NTRI pounded estimates sending the stock from $51 to $68. The table on the previous page shows expectations before and after the March quarter was announced.

- **Intuitive Surgical (ISRG)** beat the street in October 2004 when it came out with profits of $0.17 instead the $0.08 estimate. I bought ISRG that day, after the stock broke out, and watched it go from $29 to a high of $139 in 16 months. To the right you can see big spikes up that ISRG makes during 2005. Those occurred on days ISRG beat the street.

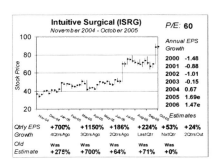

Above: Intuitive Surgical had an exceptional record of beating the street.

- In **Google's (GOOG)** first quarter as a public company, it beat the street by 14 cents, 2004 earnings estimates got increased from $2.27 to $2.52, 2005's to $3.39 from $2.81. The next quarter GOOG beat by 19 cents, after upping by 13 cents, and then 2005 estimates increased from $3.92 from $3.39. The very next quarter, Google beat by 38 cents, after estimates got upped by 12 cents twice before. 2005 estimates got upped to $5.15 from $3.92 (which was up from $3.39 and $2.81 before that). The very next quarter GOOG beats by 15 cents (which was upped previously by 13 cents and 25 cents) and 2005 got upped to $5.61 (from $5.15, $3.82, and $2.81) as 2006 increased to $7.34 (from $6.57 and $5.07). Whew, you get the drift.

Most companies have quarters that end March 30, June 30, September 31 and December 31. Earnings season starts about a week to ten days after these dates, and lasts around a month. Most of your stock research occurs in earnings season. You have to keep up with the stocks you own, continue to track stocks you are looking to buy, and keep on the lookout for fresh new ideas.

Chapter M
Buy Stocks with Low P/Es
November 7, 2003

Stock price doesn't matter. When looking to buy a new stock, the share price is not an indicator of how cheap the stock is. If it's cheap you want, look for a low P/E ratio.

Stock Price Doesn't Matter

Say we are having a party for 24 people and we need to load up on drinks, two per person (48 in total). You go to the store and see the sign to the right. Which is the better deal? You would buy the lowest price per can (P/C), taking the P and dividing by the C. So buy two cases.

Inside the Numbers: Cans of Pop	Cans (C)			Price (P)
Six-pack	6			$1.50
Case	24			$3

When we buy into a company, we want to share the profits, and we want to know how much it will cost us to get those profits (price/earnings= P/E). The lower the P/E is, the cheaper the stock is.

Pretend you could get your hands on a magic box, one that paid you once a year, based on the amount you put in. You have a choice of two boxes. Choice One pays you $0.50 each year for every $10 you put in (no limit), Choice Two pays $10 each year on a $100 investment (no limit).

Inside the Numbers: Magic Box	Profit			Each Invest-ment
Choice One	$0.50			$10
Choice Two	$10			$100

Choice Two is the better option. $1,000 into Choice One brings $50 of profits a year, and $1,000 into Choice Two gets you $100 a year. It's easy to get caught up in liking the lower $10 price, but you'll be putting in more than $10 anyway, just as you would buy more tan one share of stock. It's the profit per what you put in that really matters.

Now that you know the rules, suppose you are retiring and want to invest in a hot dog stand, using the profits as income. Looking at the table to the right, you notice that the Nice Stand is the better

Inside the Numbers: Hot Dog Stand	Yearly Profit			Business Price
Cheap stand	$1000			$10,000
Nice stand	$5000			$20,000

deal. Instinctively, you divided the price by the annual profits to see how many years it would take you to get your investment back.

Go For the Lower P/E

Assuming all other factors are the same, such as industry, growth rate, etc, would you rather own a $50 stock that makes $2.50 in profits per year, or a $5 stock that makes $0.10 in profits per year? When looking at the P/E, we see that the $50 stock is obviously the better deal. $5,000 invested in the high-priced company earns $250 in profits. $5,000 in the low-price stock nets only $100 in profits.

Inside the Numbers: Hot Dog Stand	Profit	x	P/E	=	Stock Price
High Price Stock	$2.50	x	20	=	$50
Low Price Stock	$0.10	x	50	=	$5

Don't be concerned with owning more shares. Pay attention to the P/E, or the number of years it would take to earn your money back, assuming you took the profits. In reality, we won't take the profits, the company will reinvest them to grow the business, just like using your hot dog stand profits to buy more stands. Some companies will pay part of the profits back to the people who own their stock in the form of dividends, but these are often older, more mature, companies that provide little growth opportunity. They're like the hot dog stands on every street corner.

Low-priced Stocks Are Bad News

One misconception is that low-priced stocks move faster than high-priced ones. When a $2 stock goes up $1, it gains 50%. It could also go down $1, and you've lost half your money. Penny stocks are companies that usually lose money. I don't need somebody else losing my money; I can do that myself. It would be better to own a $32 stock for a long time, and have it split two-for-one on four separate occasions. Your cost basis would then be $2 a share. When we looked at **Microsoft (MSFT)** in Chapter Two, Chart One showed MSFT at $2.30 a share after splits. At the time, MSFT was $76 a share. If lower-priced stocks actually gave a higher return, wouldn't every CEO keep splitting their company's stock until it reached $1 a share?

Many institutional money managers prefer a higher-priced share. Funds have millions of dollars to invest in each stock they buy. Getting 2,000 shares of a stock and investing $1 million is considered a positive. On the other hand, if they wanted out of a penny stock in a hurry, it might be tough finding a buyer for such a huge number of shares.

The Story of NVR (NVR)

In the early 1990s, the housing market slowed, when interest rates rose and land prices declined. **NVR Inc (NVR)**, a homebuilder, owned too much land at the time, and ended up declaring bankruptcy in 1992. With all the uncertainty, NVR stock fell below $1 a share and was $10 a share when the company emerged from bankruptcy in 1993.

NVR recovered from bankruptcy and built back profitability by changing the way it held land. NVR now purchases options on land. Options give the company y the right to build homes, but doesn't have to put its own money into the land until the lot is ready for building – and when I buyer is found. Then NVR quickly builds the home.

NVR's stock, as well as the entire homebuilding sector, turned up just as the tech stocks and the overall market turned down in 2000. There was a changing of the guard. The tech sector went out of favor and the homebuilders picked up the slack. High P/Es were out and low P/Es were in. The smart money lightened up on tech, and moved into the area where growth was to be found.

The Stock Price Had to Go Up

The best thing about stocks with low P/Es and high profit growth is these stocks can get forced higher – there's no choice but up.

NVR was $10 per share at the beginning of 2005, selling for around ten times what it would make that year (the P/E was 10). By 2000 the company would be making more in profits in a single year than the $10 stock was selling for in 1995. There's no way the stock price could be less than the yearly profits of the company, so NVR's stock was forced higher. Easy money.

In 1999, NVR was trading between $38 and $58. Had you bought at $48, you would have owned

Inside the Numbers: NVR	Profits
1995	$1.07
1996	1.72
1997	2.18
1998	4.97
1999	9.01
2000	15.30
2001	24.86
2002	36.05
2003	48.39
2004	66.42
2005	89.61

part of a company that would make $49 in profits during the next three years – and $48 in the fourth year alone.

NVR's (NVR) Stock Price Didn't Matter

Chart One is NVR's one-year chart as of May 2001. Here's what we should have been investing in, back in 2000. At the time, all the homebuilders were breaking out. I could have bought NVR for $85 a share in 2000. By 2005, it was making more than $85 a year in profits.

Chart Two shows the next 12 months of NVR. Had I bought at $200 a share in Chart One, I would have needed to sit patiently with the stock as it digested its previous gains. At one point, the stock fell to $126, losing more than 40% of its value. Dumping the stock then would have been pointless. NVR was selling for only five times what the company would make in profits that year.

In **Chart Three**, when NVR was trading for around $500 a share – earning about $50 in profits – the P/E was 10 (500/50 = 10). If the stock had split ten-for-one, it would have been a $50 stock making around $5. Either way, the stock would be selling for 10 times profits. $5,000 worth of stock would still be worth $5,000.

Normally, companies that grow profits this rapidly have the benefit of a rising P/E. But cyclical industries like homebuilding, steel, autos or commodity related areas have profits that can fall inexplicably. After 2000, the market felt that homebuilders would go through a cyclical downturn, so NVR stock went up only as much as its profits did.

Inside the Numbers: NVR	Profits		P/E		Median Stock Price
1995	$1.07	x	9	=	$9
1996	1.72	x	6	=	11
1997	2.18	x	10	=	21
1998	4.97	x	7	=	36
1999	9.01	x	5	=	48
2000	15.30	x	6	=	85
2001	24.86	x	7	=	171
2002	36.05	x	8	=	292
2003	48.39	x	9	=	419
2004	66.42	x	9	=	594
2005	89.61	x	9	=	795

What to Buy

NVR shows you can make money in a bear market. Buy stocks with rapidly-growing profits, in hot sectors with low P/Es. NVR broke out at $61, as profits were up 60% in the previous quarter.

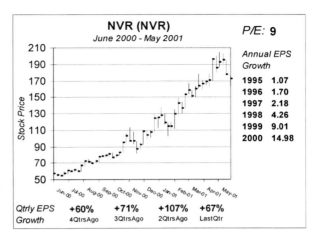

When to Buy

Here is a perfect example of when to buy. NVR based for six months, then burst to a new high – that's when to buy.

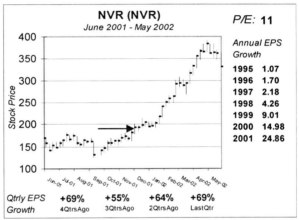

When to Hold

NVR went from $10 to $700, from 1996 to 2005. The high price scared small investors, but not smart ones. Stock price really doesn't matter – it's what you get in return.

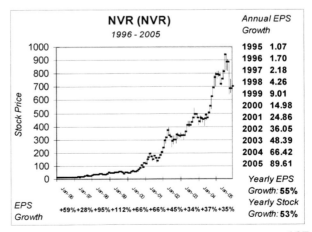

Chapter N
What Not to Buy

July 2, 2004

When I look back at my biggest mistakes I made investing in stocks, I found that semiconductor stocks, also known as microchip or chip stocks, have let me down time and time again. With so many investment choices, I found that it's best to throw in the towel on the entire sector and search for stocks in other industries.

One way you can beat the market is by owning the best stocks. Another way is to avoid the biggest losers, play defense, and preserve capital by avoiding big losses. By avoiding chip stocks, we reduce risk in our portfolio and hold more dependable stocks.

Semiconductors are too risky. These companies have not shown consistency in their earnings history; there is no certainty that the semiconductor companies will come through with the profit growth that Wall Street expects. Competition is fierce, there is little product differentiation, and chip-making-machines (also known as capital equipment) are extremely expensive. Lastly, the companies are constantly fighting Moore's Law.

Moore's Law

In 1965, Gordon Moore, co-founder of Intel, made the observation that the number of transistors per square inch had doubled every year since 1961, the year that the integrated circuit was invented. In layman's terms, he predicted that chips would become cheaper as time passed. The current version of Moore's Law holds that data density, or chip capacity, will double every 18 months or so. In a nutshell, you can get double the power for the same price, or get the same power for half the price, in only 18 months. This is why DVD players, which I remember cost $200 a few years ago, now sell for $50 or so.

Moore's Law puts tremendous pressure on chip manufacturers, since the companies have to push out twice as many chips as they did 18 months ago just to bring in the same amount of revenue. It's like they're paddling up-stream in a current that keeps getting faster and faster.

Another thing that stinks is that chip inventory gets built up. If **Proctor & Gamble (PG)** makes too much Tide, it sticks the overage in a warehouse until sales pick up, and the product can be shipped out. If PG has to store the detergent for two years, the price of Tide would still probably go up anyway. Maybe it's only a dime or a quarter more, but it's still higher. Compare this to a semiconductor manufacturer. If microchips have sat on the shelves for two years, they might be worth half what they were originally worth, if they're lucky. That is, assuming the chips aren't obsolete by then.

Rock's Law

It gets worse. Arthur Rock, a venture capitalist who originally invested in Intel to get the company started, came up with Rock's Law. Rock's Law states the cost of capital equipment (the machines used to manufacture the semiconductors) will double every four years.

Imagine how hard it would be to run our hot dog stand when every 18 months, we either have to sell twice the number of hot dogs for half the price, or sell double-sized hot dogs twice for the same price. In any case, the grills we use to cook the dogs are doubling in price every four years.

With the hot dog stand example, your main costs are in food and labor; in the semiconductor arena, the main costs are equipment. Fabrication plants cost $2 billion to $3 billion each. By 2007, the price of building a plant is expected to reach $6 billion. "Your equipment costs are the largest part of your operating budget. Your labor costs are immaterial," said Chuck Byers, director of worldwide brand management at Taiwan Semiconductor Manufacturing Co. He compares semiconductor manufacturing to "doing the pyramids backward," in "A Fab

Construction Job" (Cnet News.com, Jan. 22, 2003). Sounds like a tough way to make a buck.

Also, most companies use their profits to grow their businesses, which should bring even greater profits. **Walgreen's (WAG)** has done a great job using profits from established locations to build new stores, which bring in additional profits. In the semiconductor industry, profits are used to purchase newer capital equipment, replacing older models so the firms can keep up with newer technology. The companies are "spinning their wheels," since this equipment has to be replaced on a regular basis, draining the cash that is needed for growth and expansion.

Little Product Differentiation

Who makes the chip inside your cell phone? What about your DVD player? Does it matter? Nope. Within the semiconductor industry, there is little product differentiation. When a company came up with a new chip, competitors swooped in, figured out how the company did it, and copied the technology. This is what happened when **Nvidia (NVDA)** introduced the superior graphics chip for use in the Microsoft Xbox. The leading capital equipment manufacturer, **Applied Materials (AMAT)**, makes most of the equipment the chip companies use, so the machines that make the chips can be identical. To generate demand, there is no choice other than to lower prices, since many companies can make the same type of chip. Price decrease leads to price wars, bringing down profitability for everyone in the sector.

Semiconductors Have Little Certainty

Cell phone manufacturers, telecom equipment makers, and electronic equipment companies have a lot of choices when it comes to semiconductor companies. Chip prices tumble when inventories build up. The chip companies know that money is slipping away when product sits in the warehouses, so it's imperative to get it outta there.

When inventories are high and prices are falling out of bed, profits for semiconductor stocks can come in drastically below expectations, as in 2001 and 2002. The companies in the table to the right were some of the fastest growers during the tech boom of the late '90s, profit-wise and stock-wise. But when chip prices fell after 1999 by

Chips didn't come through as expected	Year	Profit est.	Actual Profit
Altera (ALTR)	2001	$1.25	0.33
	2002	0.25	0.23
Applied Micro (AMCC)	2001	0.53	0.49
	2002	-0.17	-0.19
Nvidia (NVDA)	2001	0.63	0.63
	2002	1.01	1.08
P M C Sierra (PMCS)	2001	1.70	-0.37
	2002	-0.21	-0.27
Silicon Storage (SSTI)	2001	2.50	0.13
	2002	0.17	-0.16
Xilinx (XLNX)	2001	1.23	1.08
	2002	0.21	0.15

as much as 90%, profits plummeted. I know because I owned them. The only company in this group that came through as expected was **Nvidia (NVDA)**.

Semiconductors Lack Consistency

To the right is a table of **Texas Instruments (TXN)**. Its alarming people reward the stock with a nice high P/E as the company has an erratic history of growing profits for shareholders. When I wrote this piece in 2004, the company earned the same amount of profits in the latest year (2003) as it did nine years earlier!

Inside the Numbers: TXN	Profit		P/E		Median Stock Price
1994	$0.48	x	10	=	$5
1995	0.70	x	10	=	7
1996	0.18	x	39	=	7
1997	0.51	x	25	=	13
1998	0.45	x	36	=	16
1999	0.92	x	42	=	39
2000	1.22	x	55	=	67
2001	0.12	x	308	=	37
2002	0.22	x	114	=	25
2003	0.48	x	48	=	23
2004	1.05	x	25	=	26
2005	1.34	x	21	=	28

Don't Buy Chip Stocks

Chart One is Texas Instruments just before the NASDAQ peaked in March 2000. Quarterly profits for the last four quarters are shown across the bottom. As you can see here, stellar profit growth among the major tech stocks spurred the NASDAQ's miraculous run to 5,000. There are two warning signs in this chart. The first one is that the sky-high stock almost quadrupled in a year. The second is that TXN had a high P/E. One clue to trouble ahead is the company's lack of consistency in growing profits each year (*Annual EPS Growth*). Stocks with high P/Es in cyclical industries are dangerous. But of course, I didn't sell my TXN.

Chart Two shows TXN the year after the market peaked in March 2000. The stock kept falling even though profits continued to rise. This is why I don't like chip stocks: they don't follow the rules of stocks that fit the mold. This chart shows annual profits are expected to fall from $1.22 too $0.81, but this news came out after the stock had already declined, and people rode it down. Also, with a high P/E of 38, either the stock's going to continue to fall, and profits are going to bounce back quick, or the stock is due for many back-and-forth years until profits can catch up to the stock price.

Chart Three shows why TXN was declining in the first place. In *Annual EPS Growth* on the right, TXN earned a paltry $0.12 in 2001 — 85% less than the $0.81 we were expecting in March of that year (shown in Chart Two). Also, the ten-year stock chart is wild, with big swings up and down. Sure, the stock grew 19% a year during this decade, but that's only because the P/E got bigger. The stock growth was not deserved.

When to Sell

This was the time to sell TXN – although you wouldn't have known at the time. The numbers still look great except for the high P/E.

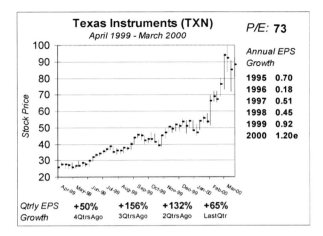

Texas Instruments (TXN)
April 1999 - March 2000

P/E: **73**

Annual EPS Growth	
1995	0.70
1996	0.18
1997	0.51
1998	0.45
1999	0.92
2000	1.20e

Qtrly EPS Growth	+50% 4QtrsAgo	+156% 3QtrsAgo	+132% 2QtrsAgo	+65% LastQtr

When to Sell

Profits are still growing faster than 20%, but the stock fell anyway—that's why I don't like semiconductors. Note 2001 profits are expected to fall (right).

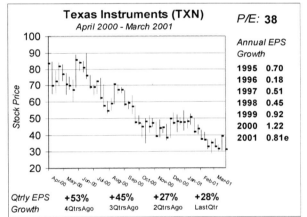

Texas Instruments (TXN)
April 2000 - March 2001

P/E: **38**

Annual EPS Growth	
1995	0.70
1996	0.18
1997	0.51
1998	0.45
1999	0.92
2000	1.22
2001	0.81e

Qtrly EPS Growth	+53% 4QtrsAgo	+45% 3QtrsAgo	+27% 2QtrsAgo	+28% LastQtr

When to Sell

The sell signal was when profits fell in 2001, well after the stock dropped. TXN didn't see $40 again, as the ten-year chart is littered with red.

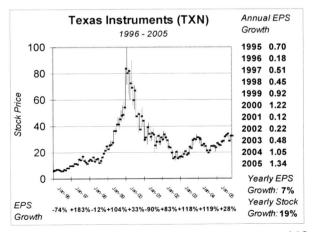

Texas Instruments (TXN)
1996 - 2005

Annual EPS Growth	
1995	0.70
1996	0.18
1997	0.51
1998	0.45
1999	0.92
2000	1.22
2001	0.12
2002	0.22
2003	0.48
2004	1.05
2005	1.34

Yearly EPS Growth: 7%
Yearly Stock Growth: 19%

EPS Growth: -74% +183% -12% +104% +33% -90% +83% +118% +119% +28%

Even though TXN's stock went from $5 to $28 in ten years, it's not a good stock. The company is benefiting from an inflated P/E — one I believe it doesn't deserve. Many investors are gambling on a pickup in technology demand, hoping that the stocks will regain their past glory. Looks like too much of a rollercoaster ride for me.

Chip Stocks Are Too Risky

The combination of low certainty and a lack of consistency in profit growth make chip stocks too risky for the small investor. There is a lot of unknown data to digest when analyzing this sector, including inventory levels in Asia, book-to-bill ratios, and daily spot-pricing. I think you have to be an industry insider to invest in chip stocks with confidence: a salesman at a semiconductor company, a vice president at a cell phone or computer manufacturer, or have the pulse on what's going on within the industry in some way. Buy what you know. Don't buy what you don't know.

Are They Really Making Any Money?

Chip companies use two accounting tricks to boost earnings. First, they write off inventory, which they claim is worthless, only to sometimes sell these same chips later on. Since the write-offs are often characterized as "one-time charges," the street often overlooks these losses when calculating annual profits during the bad years. Reports can vary from different research firms. For example, Value Line had **Cypress Semiconductor (CY)** losing $0.30 in 2002, but First Call had them losing $2.02 a share, which probably included some charges. Eventually, when the scrapped goods are sold, the entire sale is pure profit, since the cost-of-goods-sold figure is, at that point, zero. Forbes magazine reported in their article, "Dead Cat Bounce" (Oct. 13, 2003), that **Altera (ALTR)** had a $155 million charge-off in 2001. It has sold $18 million of this inventory in 2002, and another $18 million by Oct. 13, 2003.

Semiconductor companies also issue a significant amount of stock options to employees, a policy which dilutes shareholder value. The option plan at Cypress is so big that if all options were exercised, employees would own a fourth of the company ("Cypress Has Too Many Options," Forbes, Mar. 31, 2003). By giving options to employee, companies could save on overhead by paying lower salaries, thus creating the impression of higher profitability. To keep options from bring down earnings-per-share, the firms use cash to buy back their own company stock, which takes money away that might normally be used to grow the business.

Q&A

During the year 2000, I was a financial consultant for a national full-service brokerage firm. At the firm's annual conference that year, we had an opportunity to meet the main guys from the head office and participate in a Q&A. I was exited to talk with the experts, since we usually only see them on CNBC.

As questions went around the room, I wanted to ask about Texas Instruments. TXN had just broken support at $60 and went into the 50s – it broke out to the downside. This is a sell signal, shown in the middle of Chart Two a couple pages back.

So I asked, "What do you think of the chip stocks like Texas Instruments?" One of the top guys took the question and said, "Well, you need to buy these things now, because in a few years, they are going to be much higher than they are today." The next question was asked, and as it was being answered, I raised my hand again. A finger pointed my way, and I asked, "So when do you think the chip stocks will bottom?"

He replied, "Yesterday. Next question."

Back at the ranch, I was ridiculed for asking the same question twice. But I hadn't asked the same question twice. One was *what*, the other was *when*. Meanwhile, the brokers I worked with, who knew about charting, knew the bottom had yet to come.

Chapter O
When to Buy into the Market
January 3, 2003 and July, 1, 2005

We never know what stage of the economy we are at, but we always know what is yet to come.

One of the most frustrating things we investors go through is buying a stock that we have watched for a while, one which seemed to go up every year, only to see it go downhill.

There are a few ways to avoid this investing pitfall, such as reading the long-term chart of the stock (technical analysis) or looking at the company's financials (fundamental analysis). But one of the most helpful aids is what I call The Cheat Sheet.

The Cheat Sheet

The Cheat Sheet is my "crystal ball" that reads into the future, with much success, telling me where to invest and what to avoid in any market condition. Armed with The Cheat Sheet, you can pinpoint which sectors will be hot at any particular stage of the stock market and economic cycle. By having more money in the hot sectors, you can make more money in a bull market, and break even in a bear market.

Both the market and the economy go through cycles: they go up, peak, fall, and bottom. By being cognizant of which stage the economy is in, we can predict what the stock market will do. The stock market leads the economy, always a step ahead of what's going on today. The smart money on Wall Street knows this, and stays a step ahead.

For example, when the stock market was falling in 2000, the media was saying, "The economy is fine," and that we should stay in stocks. In reality, the stock market was actually anticipating a recession, which occurred in 2001. Then, in early 2003, after many investors gave up on stocks, the market rallied, before the economy heated back up in 2004.

The bear market during the beginning part of the nineties bottomed in October 1990, before the Gulf War started in January 1991. While many people were watching CNN and thinking depression, a number of big-name stocks broke out in the month that the war began—**Costco (COST), Microsoft (MSFT), International Game Technology (IGT)**, and **Home Depot (HD)**. Only Costco ever returned to those low levels of January 1991. The others left the station and never came back. IGT's still up around one-hundred-fold. HD's up thirteen-fold. You'd be in Microsoft around a buck.

To use The Cheat Sheet effectively, you need to have a handle on one of two things: what stage the economy is in, or what stage the stock market is in. Then, check The Cheat Sheet to see where to put your money.

I have used The Cheat Sheet since 2001. It has worked remarkably well, allowing me to help clients limit losses during the bear market of 2000-2002, and make close to 50% on their money when the market turned up in 2003. To truly understand The Cheat Sheet, you must first grasp the rationale behind it, knowing what to do at each of the four stages of the stock market.

What to Do When the Market is Declining

Get into safe companies that we have more certainty in. Market declines mean that the economy is about to pull back, so go with non-cyclical companies that will sell things either way: drug stocks, medical device companies, and pharmacies (people will still take care of their health). Also, remember, "People gotta eat," so anything food-related should hang in there as well. With the economy peaking, layoffs are just around the corner, so invest in for-profit education stocks, since many of the unemployed will decide to further their education.

One more thing. Don't listen to a stupid broker who says, "The market will come back," when it's obviously not coming back. Some brokers don't have a clue, so don't follow their leads and buy more **Cisco (CSCO)**. When the economy is in decline, the last thing that companies are thinking about is to spend more money on technology. CEO's are trying to save their skins, and they will look to spend less, not more.

Also, don't cash out and get out of the market, because by the time you notice you're in a bear market, you've already lost, and you don't want to miss out on the stocks that are going up—in the healthcare, consumer and education areas.

What to Do When the Market is Bottoming

When markets are bottoming, the economy is pulling back, and the Fed will lower interest rates to help banks, especially mortgage companies (since everybody refinances). The low interest rates help REITs, which finance property at lower rates. Since the Fed is cutting interest rates in a declining economy, investors looking for higher yields will invest in REITs. I found out in 2003 that bad, unprofitable penny stocks like **Lucent (LU)** and **Sun Microsystems (SUNW)** take off just as the market turns up. It seems like thing's can't get any worse, and these companies might make it after all.

What to Do When the Market is Rising

When the market is rising, an economic surge is on the horizon. Buy things that people will now spend more money on: cars, homes, vacations, restaurants and retailers. Start tipping your toe into tech stocks as well. When the market starts to rally, tech stocks will run hard and fast, since they usually make unpredictable moves up and down. Don't buy chip stocks.

What to Do When the Market is Peaking

Chapter O – When to Buy into the Market

When the economy is rising big ticket orders for cars and buildings started taking place, so now more raw materials are needed. Steel and aluminum stocks, as well as other commodities, go up due to the high demand. With all the production going up throughout the world, more oil is needed to feed an expanding economy, so oil drillers are hot stocks during this time period. With the pick up in business, companies are willing to spend more on advertising, and one of the main beneficiaries is Internet advertising.

Below is the Cheat Sheet. I have highlighted the best sectors for the long term in italics. These sectors you can buy stocks in, hold the stocks through up and down cycles, and still make money over the long term.

The Cheat Sheet

Stock Market is Declining	Stock Market is Bottoming	Stock Market is Rising	Stock Market is Peaking
Consumer Items	**Financials**	**Cyclical Stocks**	**Commodities**
Auto Parts	National Banks	Autos	Aluminum
Drugstores	*Poor Credit*	*Homebuilders*	Chemicals
Food	*Lenders*	*Restaurants*	Steel
Manufacturers	*Regional Banks*	Vacation Stocks	
Education	**REITS**	**Retail**	**Energy**
For Profit Schools		*Apparel Retailers*	Oil Companies
	Penny Stocks	National Retailers	Oil & Gas Drillers
Healthcare			
Drug Companies		**Technology**	
HMO's		*Internet*	
Medical Devices		*IT Outsourcing*	**Media**
		Computers	Advertising
Utilities		Networking	*Internet*
Water & Electric		Software	*Advertising*
Distrib.		Telecomm.	

The Cheat Sheet Picked
Career Education Corporation (CECO)

As the market peaked in 2000, the smart money looked at their own similar version of the Cheat Sheet, and saw Education stocks as a safe haven. This sector went on to become one of the hottest in the stock market from 2000 to 2003.

The smart money tries to stay a step ahead, using the Cheat Sheet to find winners before they make their big moves. A perfect example of this is **Chart One**, which is CECO from July 1999 to June 2000. The NASDAQ peaked in March 2000, so we should have been thinking ahead, and getting into defensive stocks as the market fell. Notice CECO broke out in May of that year—hitting all time highs when suckers like me rode down **Cisco (CSCO)**. Notice profits were up 110% in the latest quarter, when the stock broke out at $5.

In **Chart Two** we fast-forward to CECO four years later. The stock had incredible runs during the bear market of 2000-2003. If I had a Cheat Sheet and bought at the $5 break-out point in Chart One, I would have gained more than ten-fold. By this time, I thought I had missed the boat, since the economy was obviously strong. The Cheat Sheet was telling me to stay away from education stocks, since people were getting called back to work. This thesis proved true, when the stock fell from the $70s to the $40s in June 2004.

Chart Three is CECO during 1996-2005. I bought CECO in June '05, when I thought the economy was showing signs of slowing. On August 2, 2005 **Corinthian Colleges (COCO)** warned that profits would be lower than expected. I was wrong about the economy, it remained strong and I sold CECO five months later, taking an 8% loss. Since the economy was expanding, the Cheat Sheet said this was no sector to be in.

What to Buy

In 2000, the Cheat Sheet said to get into healthcare, consumer items and education. Here, CECO profits rose 110% in the latest quarter and had broke out.

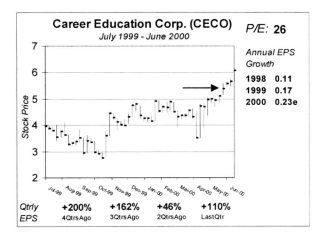

When to Sell

In retrospect, this was when to sell CECO. Everything looks great in the chart, but in four years, the stock was already up ten-fold, and the economy was strong again.

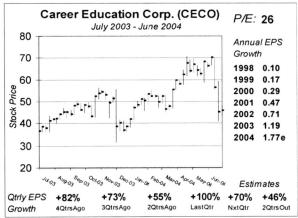

When to Sell

Here is CECO from its IPO through 2005. Although the numbers look great, the sell signal was after the climactic run in 2003 and 2004. The Cheat Sheet said sell before the fall.

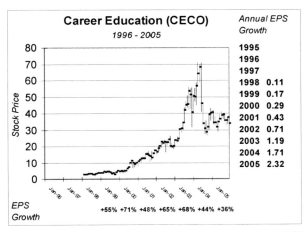

When to Buy During the Year

The end of a year brings fresh earnings estimates, bringing a powerful push to growth stocks that propels the fair value higher, and often causes them to rumble into the New Year.

When I look for the fair value of a stock, I multiply the P/E by the expected profits for that year. The data in

Inside the Numbers: ORLY	Profits		P/E		Median Stock Price
2003	$1.84	x	20	=	$37
2004	2.18e	x	20	=	44e

these two pages is from the December 2003 *Growth Stock Newsletter*. Since **O'Reilly Automotive (ORLY)** was considered a 20% grower, I consider it worth 20 times profits. In 2003, the fair value for the stock was $37 (20 x $1.84). Once we moved to 2004 numbers, the fair value jumped to $44—20% higher.

Growth stocks have more upside potential than slow growers do. **General Electric (GE)** was a $30 stock

Inside the Numbers: GE	Profits		P/E		Median Stock Price
2003	$1.56	x	19	=	$30
2004	1.70e	x	19	=	32e

projected to be fairly-valued at $32 in the next year. Not much upside, because profit growth looked minimal.

Look For Fiscal Years That End Mid-year

Companies with fiscal years ending before the calendar year ends might hit their fair value in advance. For instance, companies with fiscal year ending on December 31 are expected to hit their fair values by the end of the year. But if a company closes its books early, say June 30, then the stock could hit its fair value early.

The University of Phoenix (UOPX) was a great stock. UOPX was the online division of **Apollo Group (APOL)**. This worked great, because it allowed you to own the fastest growing part of the Apollo.

In early 2003, I was doing my homework, and I found that UOPX closed its fiscal year every June. Since UOPX ended its fiscal year six months before the calendar year, I thought the stock would hit its fair value six-months early as well.

UOPX was $51 at the time, and the fair value for 2004 was $73. I guessed UOPX would get to next years target price by June 2004, six months before the calendar year ended. UOPX hit the lofty target set for 2004, rising

Inside the Numbers: UOPX	Profits		P/E		Median Stock Price
2003	$0.93	x	55	=	$51
2004	1.33e	x	55	=	73e

43% before 2004 even arrived. UOPX was expected to grow at 35% annually, doubling in 2 years, and it had a chance to turn $10,000 into $360,000 in 10 years. Alas, APOL swallowed up UOPX, one of my best performers, took away the stock, and took away my Home Run.

The Market Runs Higher From November to April

To the right is a graph of the S&P 500's monthly performance from 1950 to 2004. Note the best months to invest are typically November through January. I believe this is caused by the ratcheting up of

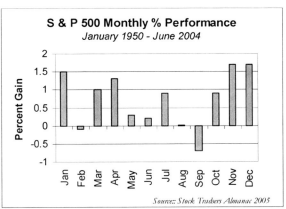

earnings estimates for the following year. Often a company's P/E stays fairly consistent. The stock growth is just a matter of the stock's price catching up to the profits.

Chapter P
When to Buy Low
December 10, 2004

How do you buy a good stock when it's down? How do you buy low? If the stock passes these six tests, the chances it will bounce back are good.

Test One: Limit Your Emotions

The first step is to take a deep breath and try to make an unemotional decision. Many of us hurry and make a rash decision that we often regret.

There are two objective ways of looking at a stock. Fundamental analysis means looking at the numbers such as profits, P/E ratio, and so on. Technical analysis means looking at the stock chart. When you're looking at a stock that's down, both the fundamentals and technicals need to be considered.

Test Two: The Trend is Your Friend

Look at a one-year view of how the stock traded for during the past year—the one-year chart.

If the stock had a wild ride throughout the year, and it's been there before, this may be normal.

A buy signal would be if the stock goes down to its old lows, then turns higher. Wait for the turn up. A stock that breaks out to a 52-week low is often bad news.

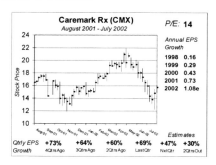

Above: Caremark was a good buy low in July 2002, because the stock had been there before. This time, CMX didn't hit a new low. CMX would go on to close in 2005 at $52 a share.

Test Three: Look for Certainty

Next, look at a long-term view of the stock – the ten-year chart.

Quality companies with steady streams of income, whether the economy is good or bad, have high certainty about the continuous prosperity of its business. Companies with high certainty should be purchased after big declines in their stock price, as long as the numbers still look good. The lower these stocks go, the better they look.

Above: Patterson Dental makes dental equipment. I'm fairly certain people will continue to get their teeth cleaned, so I feel confident buying PDCO on a dip.

Test Four: Look for Consistency

If the company has had profits up for at least five years, then there's a high degree of consistency.

If a stock has both consistency and certainty, the risk is lower, and it's good for buying on a dip.

Companies with high certainty and consistency are excellent buy-low candidates.

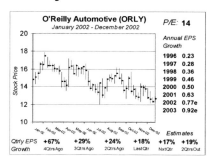

Above: O'Reilly had steady growth each year, as shown on the right of the ORLY chart. ORLY would close 2005 at $32 a share.

Beware of commodity stocks. Buy-low doesn't work well in commodity industries, because these industries usually go through a multiple-year up-cycle followed by a low, drawn out down-cycle. Don't buy commodities when they're low,; the industry could be going out of favor.

Test Five: Look for Growth Opportunity

The next step is to look at future earnings estimates.

If profits are expected to continue growing strongly, than the stock might be a great buy-low candidate.

If a company has experienced triple digit rates, the stock might correct when profit growth decelerates.

Profits can't keep doubling forever, so it's OK for a company to have profit growth rates decline as long as profits continue to grow above 20%.

Above: *American Healthways had excellent Estimates in December of 2002, making the stock a great buy low. AMHC, which later changed its name and stock symbol to Healthways (HWAY), would close 2005 at $45 a share.*

Beware of future earnings estimates in commodity businesses. Don't trust analyst earnings estimates in these businesses. Those numbers might not happen.

Test Six: Trust Your Instruments

Occasionally, good stocks get hammered unfairly and become extremely good buys. If the stock has passed the tests of consistent profit growth in the past, and if it is certain that profits will continue to grow in the future, it may not be a grand buying opportunity. It may mean the market is wrong and that the stock will bounce back.

If you already own a good stock that is down, it might be tough to swallow the fact that you might be right, and the market is wrong. You think the stock is worth $40 and it's selling for $20. If you start selling good stocks just because they are down — or because there was some bad press — you're selling yourself short. Stick to your guns. Trust your instruments.

Coventry Corrected in 2003

Test One: Limit Your Emotions

Coventry Healthcare (CVH) was an HMO I bought in 2002. I bought into CVH at $17 (the top of this chart) only to watch it drop more than a third in value to $12 in just six weeks. Then I took a step back to see what I should do. I limited my emotions.

Test Two: The Trend is Your Friend

CVH had been around $12 on four separate occasions within the last year, and at this point had not broken past the 52-week low of $10.
Verdict: Passed the test

Test Three: Look For Certainty

Coventry was an HMO, with steady revenue coming in each month as people paid their health insurance, which is important even in the worst economic conditions. Also, Coventry had recently upped 2003's forecast from $1.24 to $1.56. That announcement gave me certainty that the company was going to come through with strong profits.
Verdict: Passed the test

Test Four: Look For Consistency

To the right are the numbers on CVH I had in February 2003. Notice CVH had been growing profits each year since 1997, so there was my consistency.
Verdict: Passed the test

Test Five: Look For Growth Opportunity

Notice yearly profits were expected to jump from $1.06 to $1.56, which was 47%.
Verdict: Passed the test

Jan 2003 Inside the Numbers: CVH	Profits	P/E			Stock Price
1997	$0.03				
1998	0.22				
1999	0.29				
2000	0.38				
2001	0.55				
2002	1.06				
2003	1.56e	x	8	=	$12
2004	1.78e				

When to Buy Low—Coventry Healthcare (CVH)

Test Six: Trust Your Instruments

For eight times profits, the stock was cheap. At $12 a share, the company would probably make a third of that in profits during the next two years. I thought CVH would sell for 20 times earnings by 2004 (2004 estimates were for $1.78) and get to $36. The upside was huge, so the stock was worth the risk, and I bought.

Verdict: Passed the list

Chart One is a view of CVH in January 2003 as it dropped to $12 a share. Coventry passed the tests of certainty, consistency and growth opportunity. This stock was a good buy-low candidate.

Chart Two is the next twelve months of CVH and shows the stock not only rebounded, but also made up for lost ground.

Chart Three is a ten-year chart of Coventry Healthcare at the end of 2005. Sometimes, you have to stick to your guns and wait for the market to notice that your stock should be trading much higher.

Coventry ended up climbing this mountain through a combination of a higher P/E ratio and strong earnings growth, proving some of the best gains are made my buying a good stock when it's down.

Stick to your strategy if the stock still looks good. You will get burned once in a while, but when you're right, you'll win big, just as we did with Coventry Healthcare.

Inside the Numbers: CVH	Profits		P/E		Median Stock Price
1997	$0.03				
1998	0.22				
1999	0.29				
2000	0.38				
2001	0.55				
2002	1.06				
2003	1.83	x	11	=	$20
2004	2.48	x	12	=	30
2005	3.10	x	15	=	47

What to Buy

CVH was a solid buy in January of 2003, as the numbers looked great and the stock did not break out to a new 52-week low (it stayed above the arrow).

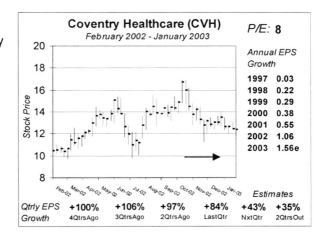

When to Buy

Here is the following twelve months of CVH. After the run higher the P/E is still low. Also, 2003 profits came in at $1.83, above the $1.56 expected in Chart One.

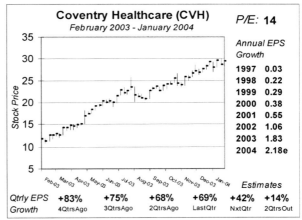

When to Hold

CVH ended up hitting that $36 target price and continued to climb through 2005, rising more than 400% off its lows.

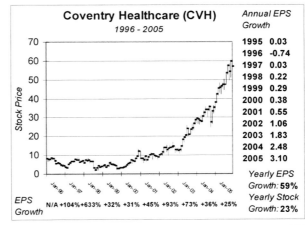

My Top Ten Stocks

One trick I use to juice returns is to buy more shares of the stocks that have strong profits and a low P/E. I kinda look at it as cheating. Since I think I'm putting more money in the best stocks, if the not-so-great stocks don't go anywhere — or go down—having more money in the winners can really help returns if I buy more low.

I have a Top Ten list. My Top Ten is what I think are my ten strongest stocks. These ten stocks take up a much higher portion of my portfolio because I think they have the ability to make serious moves higher.

Top Ten Stocks Have Huge Upside

These stocks often have profits growing at least 25%, with P/Es below the company's long-term growth rate. As we have seen, the best returns are often a combination of growing profits and the expanding P/E, so look for P/Es in the teens and the best possible growth. Coventry Healthcare became a Top Ten stock when it dropped in January of 2003, and the subsequent returns helped mask the mistakes I made in other stocks along that year.

When to Add a Stock to the Top Ten List

Sometimes I buy a stock for my Top Ten when the stock breaks out. Sometimes I buy when it's on a dip.

The biggest factor in deciding what stocks to put into the Top Ten is the amount of green I see on the chart. I take a step back and try to get an unemotional view of who the winners are. Time and time again, the stocks with the most green turn out to be the ones that have great upside. If I fiddle with the process, I often end up with a stock that's not so great in my Top Ten. I held **Chico's (CHS)** too long in 2005. It peaked, and then declined while still in the Top Ten.

As the stock rises and the P/E grows to what it should be, say 30, I sometimes sell half the position, removing the stock from the Top Ten.

Then, I look for another stock to put the proceeds into, and I move the new stock into the Top Ten.

I also remove a stock from the Top Ten if I find another that is more worthy of the big investment. Again, I sell half the shares of the stock that I'm removing from the Top Ten. By this time, the stock could have doubled in price. Selling half brings it back to equalweight position.

Mutual Funds Can't Always Make Big Bets

Many fund managers don't have the freedom to use the Top Ten technique of loading up on ten stocks.

Many funds are restricted to putting a maximum 5% of their money into any one stock. But having 10% of your money in a stock that doubles gives your portfolio a significant boost of 10%. If the other stocks in your portfolio can hold their own, or even go up, you would then have the opportunity to outperform the market.

This Knife Cuts Both Ways

Overall, the Top Ten could help or hinder your performance. It's really easy to cut your portfolio by 20% in a month by focusing on volatile stocks. For some strange reason, the top stocks are usually the most volatile, and when the market goes into a correction, these top stocks get hit the most. You would figure the best stocks would hold up the most in a bad market, but it doesn't work that way. The older stocks with low P/Es and slow profit growth like **Johnson & Johnson (JNJ)** do better in a downturn than, say, **Google (GOOG),** because many J&J shareholders hang on to it for the long term. Also, JNJ has had decades of certainty and consistency. GOOG is a young company that might lose its dominance in the search engine market, but JNJ has a stranglehold on bandages. So when the market is running on fear, GOOG is seen as a risky bet, and the stock sells off more than JNJ's. By the way, JNJ is a great stock to buy when it's low.

Chapter Q
When to Buy High

April 2, 2004

If you're gonna try to own the most powerful stocks, you have to wait until they flex their muscles. Forget the old saying, "Buy low, sell high." It will put you into loser stocks, the ones that are down — down for a reason.

In our daily routines, we are constantly trying to get a deal or save a buck. Great growth stocks are the opposite. The best stocks go up, so we must set our minds to do the opposite of what we consider normal. Think about it as paying an arm and a leg for a great piece of property, one that is likely to sell for a bucket of money down the road.

The best stocks are often high, not low. The companies are doing great. Business is booming. The stock is up. Unless you are a great value investor, don't look to the bottom of the barrel for stock picks. That's where the rotten apples are. The very best stocks go up, up and away— so search high.

There are rules to buying high. It takes a little skill and an understanding of the stock's chart pattern.

Breakouts

The key to buying high is to time the purchase accurately, and buy when it breaks out. A breakout occurs when a stock breaks through a price barrier that it couldn't overcome in the past. Say, a stock can't get past $40. One day, it bolts past $40 to close at $42 a share. This could be the highest the stock has been in months. It could be the highest it's ever been. This is the breakout.

Although it may not sound conventional, a breakout is the perfect place to buy a stock. There may be hundreds of stocks in the $35-to-$40 range. Some will go to $50, some will not. But, if a stock is going to go from $40 to $50, it must go through $41 to get there. In this example, the breakout — the buy point — is $41.

Look at it this way, if you are a staircase on the third floor of a building trying to make it to the tenth floor, going back and forth between floors two and three gets you nowhere, At some point, you have to get past that third floor.

Last Chance — All Aboard

When you see a stock break out, if it fits the mold you need to buy it. Breakouts are scary, because you are often paying the most anyone has ever paid for the stock. You might be buying after the stock is already up 10% that day. Don't be afraid of heights; just detach your emotions and stick to the program. This may be the last time the stock sees this price again, so the opportunity missed by not buying outweighs the loss which could be incurred if you sit on your hands. The best stocks don't look back, and they leave the indecisive investor sitting on his hands. Buying here separates the men from the boys.

If that stock pays off, the upside is endless. It could be worth more than all your other stocks combined. But if the stock goes to zero, the most you can lose is what you put into it. Suppose you bought 50 stocks, investing 2% of your portfolio in each stock. If one stock goes to zero, the most your portfolio can lose is 2%. But if one stock surges higher, there is no limit to the amount of money you can make.

The trick to buying on the breakout is to have your research done ahead of time. Keep a list of five to ten stocks that you like, ones that fit the mold. When one breaks out, you'll be ready to execute.

Climbing a Tree

Let's imagine your lifetime dream is to get to the top of a giant oak tree that grows in your backyard. You realize climbing straight up would be treacherous, so you devise a plan. You will climb up to one of the lower branches and build a base — like the floor of a tree house — to break your fall if you were to slip. You build the base using two-by-fours and planks; it takes you three months to build. When the first base is complete, you start heading to higher ground. Suddenly, you lose balance, and fall from the tree. Your fall is saved by the base you built. You brush off and try again. Soon, you build another base, higher than the first. You finish this base, and break out to new high ground.

This is the picture I use to illustrate a breakout. The base is the area stock tends to find when it falls. If a stock is in a range of $35 to $40, that range may be its base. If the stock breaks out to $50, then falls again, a likely stopping point will be $40. As long as the stock stays above $35, you are fine. If the stock breaks through $35, you might have trouble. Like falling from the top of the tree and missing the highest base, it might be a long way down to the next base.

It's dangerous to miss a breakout and buy after a stock has risen. It's like climbing a redwood with only one base. It's important to buy as soon as the stock leaves the base, which is the breakout point. If the stock falls back onto the base, you'll be sitting on a small loss instead of a catastrophic one.

Don't Fret If the Stock Goes Back Down

Don't get mad when you buy a stock at the breakout and see it go down. It's gonna happen. Don't change your strategy or turn into a whiner. The **GEs (GE)** or the **Proctor & Gambles (PG)** probably won't double or triple after a breakout, so you can watch these stocks and buy when they dip. Rapidly-growing companies can really make your year, so when these stocks break out, you need to make a decision then and there to buy or let the opportunity pass.

Many people suggest selling if the stock falls after a breakout. I disagree. Would you sell your new home right after you bought it, if someone offered you 90% of what you paid for it? No. If I buy a stock on a breakout, and it immediately goes down, I usually stick with it to see if it comes back. If the stock is good enough, it will find its way up again. If it continues to fall, there may have been a problem elsewhere; maybe my research failed to uncover something. Don't be afraid to buy on the breakout. If you aren't taking any losses, you're not taking enough risk.

My Biggest Mistakes Are the Stocks I Don't Buy

Number one on my breakout-miss list is **Yahoo! (YHOO)**. When the Internet stocks started taking off in 1997, I was just starting to get learn *What to Buy* and *When to Buy*. From my research, I liked Yahoo, so when it broke out in July 1997, I went to my computer to buy 100 shares, which was worth $7,500 at the time. I logged on to my E* Trade account, typed the order in my computer, and went back to look at the chart. I stared and stared, and for some reason couldn't hit the Buy button. I didn't have the confidence to make the move. I dropped the ball and didn't buy. Then, disgusted by my ineptness, I stopped watching the stock.

In January 1988, Yahoo! was taking out "Investor Fact Sheet" ads in magazines — paying for people to pay attention to its stock — and it was already on its way to making its investors 100 times their original investment, in less than three years.

The $7,500 investment I didn't make could have grown to more than $100,000. By the time the sell signal came in 2000, I was better at reading charts, and I would have been able to sell YHOO when it started to fall.

Yahoo! (YHOO) Was a Buy-High

Chart One is Yahoo during 1997. I purposely left financial data off this chart to show the power of a strong breakout. YHOO had profits up 125% and 350% during the third and fourth quarters of 1997. The arrow in Chart One points to the first breakout, the one I choked on. Also, notice the stock never falls to this level again. You are either in the stock at this point, or the train has left the station.

Chart Two shows YHOO in 1998. In this chart, we see multiple breakouts. Notice the stock breaks out to higher ground, builds a base, then breaks out again, and builds another base, breaking through once more.

I have included some financial data, but the P/E on what the stock would make in the next 12 months was not available. Still, the P/E was obviously triple-digit. At the time, the amount of money Yahoo was going to make in the future was unknown, since profits were compounding at a triple-digit rate.

Chart Three is the company during 1999. Here, we see the stock bumping its head on $50, then breaking out in November and doubling in two months. Also, notice the skyward move during November and December 1999. This is a warning sign we will discuss later. Notice all the figures are great in charts two and three.

For much of the '90s, many people thought Yahoo! was overvalued, as many Internet stocks had triple-digit P/E's. In retrospect, when Yahoo went public in April 1996, the stock sold for only 4½ times the profits it would make four years later.

Inside the Numbers: YHOO	Profits		P/E		Median Stock Price
1996	-0.01	x	N/A	=	$1
1997	0.01	x	500	=	3
1998	0.06	x	333	=	20
1999	0.12	x	583	=	70

When to Buy

Notice the stock moves back and forth during the first half of the year, then breaks through the $1.8 barrier in July. This was the breakout, when I first choked and I didn't buy.

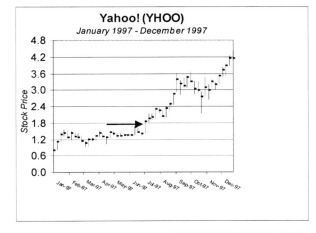

When to Buy

1998 gave me many chances to buy YHOO as the stock broke out on three separate occasions. I choked again as the stock went up 636% in the year.

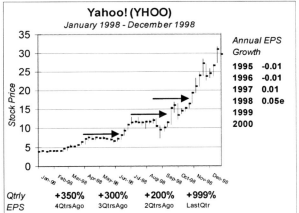

When to Buy

Year three wasn't a charm for me either, as I didn't buy YHOO when it broke out here. In three years (1997-1999), YHOO went up one hundred-fold.

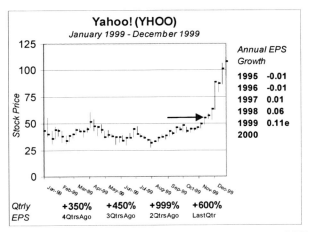

Don't Act Like a Loser While Holding a Winner

A sign of a bad investor is one who whines when the stock is bought high and drops. Thinking the purchase was bad or too high will make you want to change the way you buy stocks. You may then start buying stocks on dips, but the best stocks give few dips, so you essentially stop looking at the best stocks on the market. Don't whine if you buy a stock on a breakout and it goes down. If you can't take the heat, then get out of the kitchen, put your money in the icebox, and sit on your hands.

Winners take chances. They research what it takes to be successful, then they repeat those steps. Prior stock market winners have shown us the way, but it's up to you whether you listen or not.

Great Stocks Move Through Stages

Home Runs move in stages. The first move up is fantastic: the stock multiplies exponentially in price. Within a year you could see a double, a triple, a quadruple or more, with one to two breakouts. After I see moves such as these, I look to see what caused this move, and often find the culprit was triple-digit profit growth.

In stage two, the stock travels within a back-and-forth range — its range bound — for a period of months, a year, or even two years. Profits are still popping, but the stock can't seem to get traction. It just can't seem to break out and head higher. Being range-bound frustrates stockholders. One of my biggest weaknesses is buying a super stock after the first move. Then I'm sitting on dead money, scratching my head, wondering why the stock hasn't gone anywhere.

Stocks get stuck in a back-and-forth trading range after a big move because the supply and demand situation has changed. When a Home Run first breaks out, the news that it's super isn't out yet, because the stock has not vaulted higher. News of a stock compounding in price makes people wish they owned a stock capable of such spectacular feats. So, as investors, we often buy too high, after the first breakout, after a majority of gains have been made. At the time, we fail to recognize expectations for the stock are now high; beating the street or announcing triple-digit profit growth doesn't surprise anyone anymore. Now, investors who bought at the first breakout are looking to take profits if the stock starts to fall, as if they said to themselves, "If it falls to this price, I'm out." The lower price brings a set of sellers, which pushes the stock down more, reaching even more sellers.

Unfortunately, the stock is now down a bit, and there is upward resistance. People who bought around the all-time high are showing losses; they are underwater. Acknowledging this mistake, those who are underwater vow to "get out at even" when the stock gets back to the price it was when they bought it. Even if this stock is truly super, you still have a barrage of sellers dumping stock just before it breaks out again, sending shares lower, limiting the chances of another strong move. Since the stock does have strong profits, people buy again on the dip, pushing the stock higher once more, until another sell-off occurs at the top of the trading range. The stock is stuck in a back-and-forth pattern.

After a stock goes through a back-and-forth period, it is difficult to assume whether the stock's next big move will be higher or lower. Most stocks make two to three runs higher. If you own the stock that's in a back-and-forth basing pattern, wait with it to see what happens if the numbers are still good. If you do not yet own the stock, you have two choices: buy the stock high (when it breaks out) or buy it on a dip (if it passes the buy-low test from the previous chapter).

You will find that breakouts come in waves. Periods of many stocks breaking out are usually at the top of the bull market, or the beginning of a bear market – the most powerful ones are at the end of a bear market. Here, P/Es are low and profits are high, so these stocks are just dying to trade higher. Many great stocks will break out within weeks of the new bull market, usually when they report earnings.

Chapter R
Hold For the Long Term

September 5, 2003

Oh, hey...I meant to tell you...congratulations on your **Starbuck's (SBUX)** stock. Wow, you're in it around five, right? And your **Wal-Mart (WMT)** stock. Your family bought Wal-Mart back in the day, made so much on it, they had enough to give you a thousand shares...still not as good as putting $8,000 into **Home Depot (HD)** and having $100,000 in it...must be nice.

I know it hasn't done much lately, but **Cintas (CTAS)** has been good all these years. $4 to $40 (1990-2005). Who knew you could make so much by selling and cleaning uniforms? And now, they're in the rug business: they'll put a logo on a rug for you for, like, $100. The only catch is you have to have it cleaned by them. I just heard that Cintas will also clean your bathroom at work and sanitize the walls, for a fee, too. It's expensive, but for some people, it would be worth it.

How about that **Cognizant Technology Solutions (CTSH)?** It doubles every other year. LOL! Sweet! I know. And NOBODY talks about it.

Oh, you say you don't own those stocks...yeah, I know what you mean.

I didn't know about stocks when I was younger, I had to learn it on my own. Would have been nice to have known this earlier...but I guess they don't teach that in school. I would rather have had Stock Class than Art History or one of those stupid classes I don't even remember.

There are three reasons we don't own those really big winners of the last century, the stocks that go from 1 to 100 and *stay* over 100. Either we didn't know to look at the profits, or we knew what made the best stocks great and didn't take action. Maybe we took action and bought the great stocks, then sold them before they would have made us rich.

When I look for potential new additions to the portfolio, I always look for the perfect situation. The perfect situation for me is to find one of those wonderful stocks that you usually hear about after the fact, before they take off. You know which ones I mean, the stocks that make regular people millionaires. The kind of stock that you buy and hold, the kind that always seems to go up through thick and thin. That's the kind of stock we all dream about owning. The story of Anne Scheiber was a textbook case of success in buy and hold:

In 1944, a young lawyer named Anne Scheiber retired from her dreary job at the Internal Revenue Service. Despite her graduate degree, she was repeatedly denied promotions, and she never made more than $3,150 a year (the equivalent of about $35,000 in 2002). Still, she managed to scrape together $5,000 in savings, and she put it all into stocks.

Over the next six years, stock prices doubled, and in 1950, with her profits, she bought 1000 shares of Schering-Plough Corp., the drug company (at the time, it was called Schering Corp.), for about $10,000. It became her largest holding. When she died in 1995, those 1000 shares became, through splits, 128,000 shares, worth $7.5 million. (Schering would quadruple again in the six years after her death).

Using dividends and profits, she bought other stocks as well. Among her long-term holdings, Coca-Cola Co. increased in value from $28,000 to $720,000 during the last 15 years of her life, and that doesn't even count dividends. As a Peter Lynch-style investor, she bought Loews because she liked the movie theaters, even though the company later became a tobacco-and-insurance company. Her Loews stock was eventually worth $2.2 million at her death. Her PepsiCo stock was worth $1.6 million; Bristol-Myers Squibb $900,000; Allied-Signal (now part of Honeywell), $1 million. In all Anne Scheiber parlayed her $5000 savings into an investment account valued at $22 million.

Then she gave it all away to the startled folks who ran Yeshiva University in New York. She never attended Yeshiva, but every weekday morning, in her frugal way, she read the Wall Street Journal in its library. She was grateful. How did she do it? Nothing special. "She just held onto what she bought and never sold anything," her broker, William Fay of Merrill Lynch, said after she died. "She believed in these companies. She just stayed with them. She didn't care if the market was up or down." All of her stocks went through rough patches - all of them. There was a time, "during the '70s when Schering dropped off and lost half its value," Fay said. But Scheiber didn't sell during the inflation and recession of the 1970s. She held through it all: the Kennedy assassination, the Korean War, the Cold War, the oil embargo.... She held.[4]

I once had a client. Well, I can't really say he was a client. He just wanted to put some stocks in our brokerage firm for safekeeping. About five stocks in total: **Bell South (BLS), Kimberly Clark (KMB), Proctor & Gamble (PG),** and another one I can't remember. He was a simple man, who lived in the same suburb of Memphis as I did. You wouldn't be able to tell he was a millionaire. I think I blew him off the first time he came in the office. He was walking around outside, without a car around, and decided to walk in our door and ask some questions. I think he said his wife was somewhere near.

It's been years, but I think his Kimberly Clark stock was worth more than $100,000. It was his smallest position. PG was the biggest, I think. BLS I remember being more than $300,000, but I'm just guessing.

Something happened to this man. Somehow, somebody showed him the Secret Code of buying stocks. Scratch that, owning stocks. The difference was that he held his stocks. He was in his seventies or eighties, so I guess he could have learned it on his own. I tried to get him to sell some Kimberly Clark and buy **Cisco (CSCO),** after it fell 10% from its high in 2000. That would have been a mistake.

---

[4] *from "The Secret Code of the Superior Investor" by James K. Glassman. Random House, 2002.*

I did a reverse lookup on my computer to see how much he would have had to invest in each stock 30 years ago to accumulate such wealth. In each case, it was around $1,000. The trick to owning a big winner isn't that you bought the stock; it's that you didn't sell it.

It is better to pass stock on to your children than it is to pass money. They will have an inclination to hold a stock, but they will probably spend the money. Hopefully, you'll have a good broker, and the broker will show them, "You're in this stock at $2 a share, and now it's $75." Then, the goal is to get to $100. If you give cash to your heirs, they might spend it or waste it. People have no personal bond with mutual funds, no emotional attachment, but they have a connection with a retail stock they shop with.

The main reason people don't own long-term winners is that they lack patience to hold stocks for the long term. The stock market repeats itself, showing us what to buy, when to buy and when to sell, but some of us are too stubborn to learn from the past, and continuously dump great stocks without giving them a chance. The ego is too powerful to reason with, and it makes million-dollar mistakes.

One of the greatest long-term winners of our time is **Amgen (AMGN)**. AMGN's drug EPOGEN© was licensed for marketing on June 1, 1989, giving the stock growth opportunity. The drug was highlighted in *Businessweek's* "Products of the Year" and "Best of 1989" issues.

In Amgen's numbers, the things that stand out most are Amgen's profits from 1989 to 1992, and its stock price, which went up ten-fold in only four years. Then the profit growth rate slowed, as did the stock's growth rate. It took 13 years for both to go up ten-fold once more. In between, the company never had a down year of profits, so a true sell signal for long-term shareholders never occurred. Amgen's profits and stock both went up one hundred-fold in 16 years, yet few investors stuck around and waited.

Hold Amgen (AMGN) for the Long Term

Amgen's run to greatness started back in March 1990. **Chart One** shows AMGN, as it started to make its big move. At the time, it looked like AMGN was trading for 50-times profits, but the company ended up blowing away estimates, so when all was said and done, the P/E was only 15 at the breakout. In the last quarter of this chart, AMGN started selling NEUPOGEN© after receiving approval from the FDA.

Chart Two shows AMGN at its low point of the 2000-2002 bear market. At one point, the stock lost over 40% of its value in only three months. But on the right, profits are up each year. This kind of consistency gives investors more certainty that there will continue to be growth opportunity in the future. This was not a stock to give up on. People who became overcome with fear and sold marked the bottom for this stock.

Chart Three shows AMGN's ten-year chart. As fear among investors caused many to jump ship (at the bottom) it was as though the stock was waiting for the whiners to bail before it turned higher. One reason the stock turned up in 2002 was profit growth accelerated.

Inside the Numbers: AMGN	Profits		P/E		Median Stock Price
1989	$0.02	x	43	=	$0.80
1990	0.08	x	28	=	2
1991	0.16	x	36	=	6
1992	0.26	x	31	=	8
1993	0.31	x	17	=	5
1994	0.39	x	16	=	6
1995	0.48	x	21	=	10
1996	0.60	x	24	=	14
1997	0.69	x	20	=	14
1998	0.82	x	20	=	16
1999	0.99	x	37	=	37
2000	1.05	x	62	=	65
2001	1.18	x	51	=	60
2002	1.39	x	47	=	47
2003	1.90	x	32	=	60
2004	2.40	x	25	=	59
2005	3.20	x	23	=	72

When to Buy

Here is AMGN's breakout in 1991. Each quarter in this chart shows triple-digit profit growth. The arrows point out two buy-points, which were both breakouts to new highs.

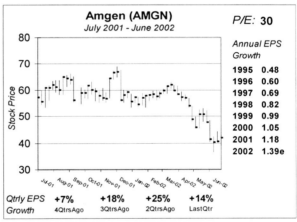

Amgen (AMGN)
April 1990 - March 1991

P/E: 68

Annual EPS Growth

Year	EPS
1985	0.001
1986	0.002
1987	0.002
1988	-0.010
1989	0.02
1990	0.08

Qtrly EPS	+167%	+833%	+113%	+328%
	4QtrsAgo	3QtrsAgo	2QtrsAgo	LastQtr

When to Hold

Although this looks like a time to sell, AMGN had already proven itself as a long-term winner. This correction proved to be a low point for the stock.

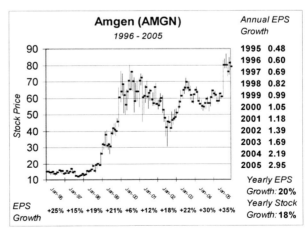

Amgen (AMGN)
July 2001 - June 2002

P/E: 30

Annual EPS Growth

Year	EPS
1995	0.48
1996	0.60
1997	0.69
1998	0.82
1999	0.99
2000	1.05
2001	1.18
2002	1.39e

Qtrly EPS Growth	+7%	+18%	+25%	+14%
	4QtrsAgo	3QtrsAgo	2QtrsAgo	LastQtr

When to Hold

Investors that bought Amgen when it broke out in 1990, and held on, now have a cost basis in the stock of $1.25 a share.

Amgen (AMGN)
1996 - 2005

Annual EPS Growth

Year	EPS
1995	0.48
1996	0.60
1997	0.69
1998	0.82
1999	0.99
2000	1.05
2001	1.18
2002	1.39
2003	1.69
2004	2.19
2005	2.95

Yearly EPS Growth: 20%
Yearly Stock Growth: 18%

EPS Growth	+25%	+15%	+19%	+21%	+6%	+12%	+18%	+22%	+30%	+35%

145

AMGN is a great example of how you can be wrong about when to buy a stock, but right on the stock to buy, and still be in good shape, since the profits will eventually bail you out. Say, you bought AMGN at its high in 2000. You would have paid $80 for it, only to watch the stock go all the way down to $30 by the summer of 2002. The stock came down in a bear market. But since profits kept growing the whole time, Amgen stock bounced back, hitting new highs and popping its head over $80 in 2005. Sure, it took a while to get there. But in 2005, the 24 P/E was a lot lower than the 62 figure in 2000. We could see bigger gains ahead for Amgen during the next five years, as the P/E could enlarge.

The Key to Owning Long-Term Winners

A key to owning stocks which make big gains over long periods is to buy the stock at the beginning of a long run, typically when it breaks out. It's important to make big gains in the stock right away so you can rationalize holding the stock in periods when it doesn't go up.

For instance, say you buy a stock at $20, and in a year, it climbs to $30. If the stock does nothing the second year, it's OK in your mind, since you have still made 50% on your money. If the stock then rises to $40 in year three, you have doubled your money in only three years, averaging 24% along the way, using Sharek's Rule of 72. Nice job.

New investors often get sucked into the gambling game of stocks. In this game, we try to make money on one trade, then sell the stock and try again. Make 20% here, lose 20% there, and maybe make 20% on the third try. This works if you are really good, but the rest of us might be better off letting the power of compounding work for us. Trading stocks is difficult because you have to constantly cut losses, consistently monitor your portfolio, giving up quality of life, and keep the emotions out of it. All for what? To make 20% in the next Amgen?

When you trade stocks, a healthy percentage of your trades has to be winners. When you buy and hold great stocks, you may find one stock that goes up four-fold in price, so you can make money with a tiny success rate (because you're hitting Home Runs). How hard would it be to trade your way to four-times your investment?

If you buy a stock during a back-and-forth period, after a big run has been made, you could get bored and sick of wasting your time. You might sell a great stock. If you happen to buy a stock and it goes nowhere for months, try to stick with it if it still fits the mold. Hold out for the next big move; you've earned it. If you sell, you'll probably avoid buying the stock again, because you might be convinced that it's dead money, and miss out on a real good opportunity.

I always try to buy a stock at the beginning of a run and purposely hold it way too long, then have stocks in different growth stages. Some stocks are rising right now, some are taking a breather, and some are coming down. I usually add new picks when they break out, so I could try and get a quick head start. Then, when the stock enters a stagnant period, I look for another stock to buy, one that's breaking out. All the while, I'm hanging on to our first buy (which does nothing for a year or so, after running up). I would hopefully make money on the second stock to boost the whole portfolio. Then, after being on the back burner, the first stock breaks out again and runs to new highs. When a stock is on the back burner, I may not keep up with its news headlines as much as when I first bought it, but I definitely make sure it still fits the mold. Eventually, something will happen to mess up our perfect world, like a company lowering earnings estimates, but there is another stock around the corner waiting to take its place.

Investors with portfolios that are down a bunch have a chance to get their portfolios back to even, by holding great stocks for the long term. It probably won't be with AMGN, but it could be with another stock that fits the mold and is held for the long-term. Great stocks — even good stocks — have inexplicable runs that could span 10 to 20 years. The key is to hold the stock for the long term and let the power of compounding work its magic.

Chapter S
Don't Expect Consistent Returns

August 6, 2004

One of the biggest mistakes I see people make is grading how much their holdings have gone up during a certain time period. They often want to know how much their portfolios have gone up year-to-date, and how much each stock is up or down from the original purchase price.

Don't Time Your Stocks With a Stopwatch

As a stock investor, timing your stocks is your single biggest obstacle – one some people aren't objective or rational enough to overcome. It is so easy nowadays to get online and compare your portfolio to the Dow, the NASDAQ, or the S&P 500. Unfortunately, doing so is like taking a stopwatch to a marathon runner, and timing him on what he does during a 40-yard section at the beginning of a marathon.

Stocks are not going to give you consistent returns, even though we wish they could. We sometimes obsess and make radical moves if our stock or portfolio hasn't done what we wanted, when we wanted it to.

Successful stock investing doesn't have a rule that says your favorite stock has to go up a certain percentage each year. If you have a stock that grows 12% a year, it would be nice to see it go up 1% a month, but it won't. There will be months it might go up 5%, down 5%, up 2%, down 20%, then maybe up 40%. Even on a yearly basis, you can't expect consistent returns. There will be years the stock has 20% losses and others with 50% gains.

There will be incredible amounts of volatility in your stock portfolio. Believe it or not, there will be months in which your whole stock portfolio falls 20%. If you can't take the volatility, get out of the market. Don't blame the stock or the stock market for your insecurities.

When the NASDAQ drops 20 points in a day, it's a 1% loss. The whole NASDAQ market, which includes the stocks in your portfolio with four letter symbols, loses 1% in only a day. Just like that. If that goes on for five days, back-to-back, it's around a 5% loss in only a week. Sounds like too much volatility? You can avoid volatility by staying away from the stock market. Just don't own stocks. Then, you don't get the opportunity to, say, quadruple your money in 10 years. Using Sharek's Rule of 72, that's a 14.4% yearly return.

Why Pick January 1?

As you evaluate your stock portfolio, do not fall into the trap of timing your stocks on what they did during a calendar year. A "year" does not carry any statistical evidence that says you will get a fair price, at the beginning or the end of the year. There's no bell that rings and tells each stock to get back to where it should be by January 1. Many companies don't even end their fiscal year on December 31. Some have a March year-end, some June 30.

Imagine you could go back to mid-1983 and buy **Wal-Mart (WMT)**. What do you do when it slides 40% by early 1984? Do you sell? Let's say you do. When the market turns up, do you really think you would jump back into a stock you just lost 40% on? Probably not. You probably would have bought WMT at around $1.40 a share and sold out for under a buck. Sucker. You could be holding the best hand, and fold before even looking at the cards.

Still, I know a number of whiners that always time their portfolio to the market. When the NASDAQ and the tech stocks were running out of control, these investors wanted to be there. When the market subsequently went down, they changed their tune and compared the portfolio to what they could have earned in CDs at the bank. Then they sell, sometimes fabulous stocks, making a life-long mistake, the kind of mistake you never recover from. First, they may have sold the winning lottery ticket before the drawing. Even if this proved to be true, they rarely get back in, because their ego won't allow it. Second, they sear into their brains that owning stocks with great profits does not work, which is absolutely preposterous.

The Market

One of the worst mistakes an investor can make is selling a great stock when the market is down. Most great stocks go down in poor markets. These leaders often are the most volatile, losing more than a regular stock would when the market falls, then maybe doubling off their lows when the sky opens up. Conversely, safe stocks won't bounce back and forth as much, but they probably don't give superlative returns over the long run. If you own great stocks, expect your portfolio to be volatile.

The market price is just the price people are willing to buy or sell at on a particular day. When you buy a stock, you think the stock is actually worth more than it is selling for, right? I mean, that's why you bought it. You thought the market was wrong, and your stock was undervalued. A disadvantage of conveniently being able to look up stocks on the Internet is that you may get caught up in the day-to-day pricing action and get scared when the market is going down. Keep in mind: you may be right and the market may be wrong.

Look at Your Stock as You Look at Your Home

What is your house worth today? Has it gone up since you first purchased it? Probably so. If someone came to your front door and offered to buy your house for 10% off of what it was worth, would you accept it? No. What if he came back next month and offered you 80% of the home's value? What would you do? You would probably say, "No, thank you." Then, maybe you would get that fear in the back of your mind that the house is going down in value. This is similar to what happens when people check their stock prices, except that in the stock market, many people are giving opinions instead of just one individual.

Suppose a week later, the same man showed up at your house with a friend. He explained that you need to sell because the taxes were too high, you might have a crack in the foundation, and the area is going down hill. You start to sweat a little. They now offer you a deal, because they like you. They will take the property off your hands for half of what you thought it was worth a month ago. As the first man makes the offer, the second man shakes his head and says things like, "Maybe we shouldn't buy this house," which only reinforces your fear. Now what do you do? Do you sell? Well, common sense tells you not to. Selling your home to these two guys would be silly.

Your home's value bounces back and forth. You don't get your home appraised each month, since in your mind, it's a "long-term investment".

Make up Your Own Mind

To find out what a stock may be worth, try multiplying what the firm makes in profits at the rate which profits are growing. Take **Lowe's (LOW)** as an example.

Assume you bought LOW stock in 1994 for $9 a share and held it. Three years later, in 1997, you thought of selling because LOW was only $10 a share. Should you sell because the returns had been lousy?

Here's how to handle this dilemma. Look at profits during the past years, and next year's expected profits. If the company is growing consistently, this might be a case in which the market's wrong and you are right. In this example, LOW's P/E has shrunk from 26 to 20. If, in the next year, the stock's P/E comes back to 26, the stock will be right where it should be.

In reality, that's exactly what happened. By 1998, LOW's P/E came back to 26. Through a combination of a higher P/E and 33% profit growth, the stock climbed an additional 80%.

Lowe's (LOW) Did Not Give Consistent Returns

Chart One shows Lowe's during 2000. The stock market went down after March of that year, and so did Lowe's stock. Although this stock was down, quarterly profits (along the bottom) were still growing. This was an instance of *When to Buy*, not *When to Sell*.

Chart Two is LOW during 2002, another down year for the stock market. Notice the big drop in July, 2002. This is an example of the volatility you can expect in an individual stock. July 2002 was a tough month for stocks. Many stock portfolios dropped 20% – I remember everything dropping 10% that month. It's also interesting to note that LOW, with its superior profit growth, recouped lost ground within two months.

Chart Three is a ten-year view of Lowe's. From 1996 to 2005, there were multiple drops of more than 20% in a single month, and an extended period during 1998-2000, when the stock lost 40%.

Volatility caused a lot of investors to jump ship on this stock too early. When you take a step back and look at the earnings table, LOW was clearly a buy from 1996 forward. Note from 1995 through 2004, the stock's median price was always up. But if you bought at the highs in Chart One, you would have been losing money in the stock in the middle of Chart Two – more than two years later.

Inside the Numbers: LOW	Profits		P/E		Median Stock Price
1994	$0.35	x	26	=	$9
1995	0.34	x	24	=	8
1996	0.43	x	21	=	9
1997	0.51	x	20	=	10
1998	0.68	x	26	=	18
1999	0.90	x	30	=	27
2000	1.06	x	24	=	25
2001	1.30	x	27	=	35
2002	1.85	x	22	=	41
2003	2.32	x	20	=	47
2004	2.71e	x	20	=	53

What to Buy

When the stock fell in 2002, quarterly profits were still growing rapidly, so there was no need to sell the stock – LOW should have been bought then, not sold.

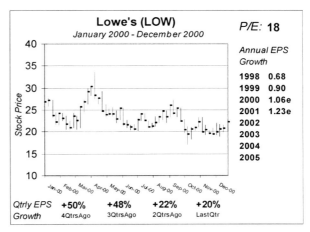

Lowe's (LOW)
January 2000 - December 2000

P/E: **18**

Annual EPS Growth

1998	0.68
1999	0.90
2000	1.06e
2001	1.23e
2002	
2003	
2004	
2005	

Qtrly EPS Growth	+50% 4QtrsAgo	+48% 3QtrsAgo	+22% 2QtrsAgo	+20% LastQtr

When to Buy

During 2002, LOW was still a good company, but it was being affected by market conditions. LOW is a good buy here with its 17 P/E.

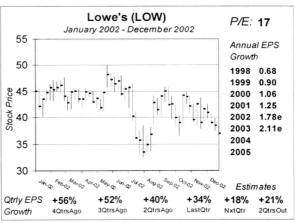

Lowe's (LOW)
January 2002 - December 2002

P/E: **17**

Annual EPS Growth

1998	0.68
1999	0.90
2000	1.06
2001	1.25
2002	1.78e
2003	2.11e
2004	
2005	

Estimates

Qtrly EPS Growth	+56% 4QtrsAgo	+52% 3QtrsAgo	+40% 2QtrsAgo	+34% LastQtr	+18% NxtQtr	+21% 2QtrsOut

When to Hold

In 2003, the stock market turned up and LOW raced to $60. Lowe's was a good stock to own, but it didn't provide consistent returns.

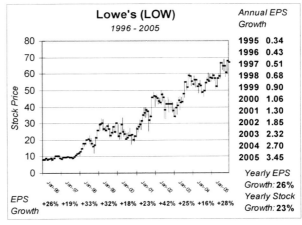

Lowe's (LOW)
1996 - 2005

Annual EPS Growth

1995	0.34
1996	0.43
1997	0.51
1998	0.68
1999	0.90
2000	1.06
2001	1.30
2002	1.85
2003	2.32
2004	2.70
2005	3.45

Yearly EPS Growth: **26%**
Yearly Stock Growth: **23%**

EPS Growth	+26%	+19%	+33%	+32%	+18%	+23%	+42%	+25%	+16%	+28%

Has the Company Changed?

When you buy stocks, what you're really doing is buying a piece of a business. You are part owner. If the market falls, and your stock also falls, ask yourself if anything has changed in that business.

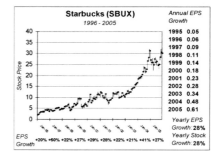

Above: Starbucks didn't provide consistent returns between 1998 and 2002.

Will the market decline keep you from going to **Starbucks (SBUX)**? If Starbucks still makes money as usual, should their company be worth any less because the market is down? No. So, if SBUX drops 30% due to market conditions, take a step back and look at the big picture.

You Are on a Different Program

If you own a portfolio loaded with stocks that fit the mold, you are on a different program than the average investor. Don't worry about the market. Great stocks can break through a bad market.

Bad markets often re-price the bad stocks to lower levels. Unfortunately, the bad market will bring down our good stocks as well. But when the market turns up — it always does — the smart money will first invest in the most attractive stocks, the stocks we should own. The first stocks to rally and break out to new highs are often stocks that fit the mold; stocks that deserved to be higher in the first place; stocks that have some catching-up to do.

The Difference Between Volatility and Losses

Don't confuse volatility with losses. This will cause you to sell at the worst possible point. The market is worst right before it turns up. Your portfolio could lose, say, 20% of its value, then suddenly drop another 10% to 20% in a matter of days or weeks. These market conditions could cause the naive investor to sell just before the market turned up. You would know the turn is coming, because you'd have a dead feeling in your stomach. You'd have given up hope and felt depressed about the situation. The whiner will sell, and then the great stocks will double by year end. It takes heart and determination to be a winner. The difference between a winner and whiner isn't in what they do when the market is going up, it's what they do when the market is going down.

Although your stock or portfolio might be showing a loss, this may just be temporary, so don't get flustered and do something stupid. If your stuff is down, confirm that your stocks fit the mold, and wait out the storm.

Don't Sell a Stock Because it Doesn't Give Consistent Returns

One of the worst financial mistakes you could make in your life is to dump your Home Run before it takes off. I have had people dump **Cognizant Technology Solutions (CTSH)**, a stock with the potential of being the **Microsoft (MSFT)** stock of this decade, because they were frustrated with their overall portfolio. Gosh, if you are going to sell, at least hang on to the superstars. Selling now could be a bigger financial mistake than going bankrupt. What could this stock be 10 years from now? Could $5,000 have grown to $50,000? If it was a Home Run, it could, and should, maybe even would.

When investors give up on great stocks, they have a conviction in their mind that they are right, and they are forceful in making this change. I guess you have to be strong to make a monumental mistake. Try with all your might to avoid this temptation, as if it were a crack cocaine addiction. By far, selling a great stock could be the worst mistake you ever make in your investing career.

Chapter T
Don't Sell Stocks that Fit the Mold

June 4, 2004

Don't Get Shaken Out

Its tough hanging on to something that's about to turn up; don't get shaken out. When we invest in stocks, the main goal is to own more down the road than we do today. Unfortunately, we are in a society where everything is graded on this, "What have my stocks done lately." We micromanage our portfolios, looking to trade in and out to make a quick buck. Sometimes we trade far too often, getting scared after the market has gone down, and we want to invest more money after the market has gone up.

What I have often wonder about **McDonald's (MCD)** is where are the people who sold MCD when the stock was at a dollar? Since the stock traded daily for decades, along the way investors sold too soon, either made a quick gain or lost money on a stock that was All-Madden.

Above: McDonald's 1987 – 1996.

Beating the Street With Home Depot

In *Beating the Street*, Peter Lynch explains he bought during "the infancy of Home Depot, with the stock (adjusted backward for later splits) selling for 25 cents a share, and I'd seen it with my own eyes and bought it, but then lost interest and sold it a year later...Imagine, a stock that goes from 25 cents to $65, a 260-bagger in 15 years, and I was on the scene at the creation and didn't see the potential."[5]

---

[5] *From Beating the Street, by Peter Lynch, 1994 pg 89, Simon & Schuster*

Below are the stocks I sold from my personal portfolio during 2002, taken straight from my 2002 tax returns. I have made so many mistakes that you can't come up with another one. Look at those gains I could have had. I am afraid to check what these would be worth now; it would make me sick.

Many people make their biggest mistakes by losing money on a stock. My

2002 David Sharek Personal Gains and Losses				
Stock	Purchase Price	Sale Price	5/27/04 Price	%Gain/loss since sale
Too	$33	21	16	-24%
O'Reilly	36	30	44	47%
Amer. Health	12	8	21	163%
Univ. Phoenix	31	30	89	197%
Autozone	83	82	85	4%
Coven. Health	24	22	45	105%
Dollar Tree	37	37	28	-24%
Holywd. Video	14	17	13	-24%
Jos. A. Bank	10	13	32	146%
Lab Corp.	45	46	41	-11%
Multmdia.Gam	17	9	22	144%
Nautilus	37	14	15	7%
Average Gain Left on the Table				61%

biggest mistake has been failing to buy stocks that gained three-fold, five-fold, or even ten-fold in price. My second biggest has been selling good stocks too soon, and missing massive gains. Looking at the table above, there were some very good stocks that I simply didn't hold long enough. I didn't give them a chance to grow. Some of the stocks were sold because their businesses declined, like **Too (TOO)** and **Nautilus (NLS)**. Otherwise, I was trying to do too much, or I didn't believe I was on the right track. If I had bought and held the above stocks, they would have gained an average of 57% in the next two years, even in a tough market. That's not even counting the fact that by biggest holding at the time, **Jos. A. Bank (JOSB)** would have made one of the biggest percentage gains.

I tried a lot of different things in 2002. I tried cutting my losses when a stock I bought would drop 10% (in which case it would drop 10%, I would sell, and the stock would take off to the upside). I tried buying in, letting a stock run way up in price, then setting a floor for which I would sell "if it hits this price." So what happened? The market would drop, I would sell, then the stock would just bounce right back.

I Got Shaken Out of My Home Run

One stock I gave up on way too soon is **Urban Outfitters (URBN)**. Urban Outfitters is a specialty retail store that sells casual clothes such as T-shirts and jeans, geared towards men and women from age 18 to 30. Kinda like trendy skateboard stuff students wear at college.

I bought URBN in my managed portfolio in April 2002. The stock went higher during the next three months, and then got boring during the second half of 2002 as it traveled slowly downward. All my gains were erased, and I was sitting with a stock that fell below the price I bought it at. It was aggravating hanging onto URBN, waiting for it to come back.

So in January of 2003, I sold Urban Outfitters at around $2.75 a share to try and make room for a hot stock. The table on the right shows URBN's numbers at the time of my sale.

When I Sold URBN in Jan 2003	Profits		P/E		Median Stock Price
2002	$0.18e	x	17	=	$3
2003	0.21e	x	12	=	2.75

In 2003, if the stock was worth 25 times profits, URBN was fairly valued in the beginning of the year at $5 (25 x $0.21 = $5). I sold at $2.75.

Don't Let a Big Winner Pass You by

Then URBN started climbing and I then made another mistake by not buying back into the stock once it started to show strength. This is one of the problems with selling a stock: if it's a true leader, you face the risk of not getting back in, then letting a big winner pass you by.

A lot of people get scared when the market pulls back. Investors want to get out of stocks. If you own the best stocks, the market can only hold back your portfolio for so long. Eventually, things turn back up.

The Best Stocks Do the Same Thing

The best stocks almost always do the same thing.

- When the market starts to decline, the best stocks don't crack under pressure at first. They hold up, or even continuing to rise in the face of the pullback.

- If the market continues to plunge, these stocks eventually break down as well, often correcting 40% or more.

- When the dust finally clears, investors realize what a steal these leading stocks are, causing the stocks to race higher.

- The best stocks quickly bounce back to their old highs, which usually takes one to two months. Stocks with high profit growth are the best ones to own during the first leg of an up market.

- Now the stock has some catching-up to do. Great stocks have the ability to double, triple, or quadruple off their lows in this case. If you have a great stock that's down 50% due to market conditions, and it gets back to that old price you originally bought at, that would be a double. If the stock doubles again (there's some catching-up to do), you have a four-fold gain from the lows.

In the case of Urban Outfitters, it was clear that the stock was being punished by the market, since profits were still growing rapidly. The P/E was half of what it should have been.

I Sold URBN Before It Went up Ten-Fold

Chart One shows URBN from February 2002 to January 2003. I added the stock to my managed portfolio on 4/10/02 at $3. At first, the stock went over $4, and it looked like I made a sound purchase. Then the stock went through a down period, slowly eating away my gains. I sold and took a small loss when it looked like profit growth would fall to 15%, ignoring the fact that URBN was beating the pants of earnings estimates.

Chart Two shows the stock the following 12 months. In early 2003, URBN beat the street and posted 27% profit growth, much better than the 15% anticipated. The stock broke out in March of 2003, the first month of the new bull market. As soon as the market turned up, the smart money started buying URBN. One of the reasons the stock jumped so much in 2003 was that it had to make up for lost ground. The stock market can hold a good stock back for only so long. Eventually, a company's profit growth prevails as the main factor in determining its stock price.

Chart Three is from 1996 to 2005. After selling out at $2.75 I was too stubborn to get back in, and missed a ten-bagger.

Looking at the numbers, there is no way I should have sold URBN. At least, I should have bought the stock back with profits growing 69% in 2003, and 53% in 2004.

Inside the Numbers: URBN	Profits		P/E		Median Stock Price
2002	$0.18	x	17	=	$3
2003	0.30	x	21	=	6
2004	0.57	x	30	=	17
2005	0.77	x	34	=	26

When I sold Urban Outfitters at around $2.75 in January 2003, the stock was selling for only the nine times the profit it would make by the end of that year.

When to Hold

This is what a good stock looks like at the end of a bear market. Profits grew strong but the stock still trended down. Low P/E in January 2003 gave URBN huge upside.

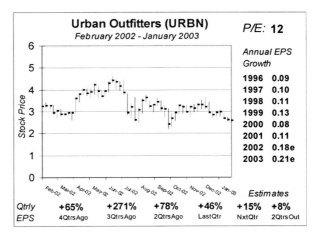

Urban Outfitters (URBN)	P/E: 12
February 2002 - January 2003	

Annual EPS Growth	
1996	0.09
1997	0.10
1998	0.11
1999	0.13
2000	0.08
2001	0.11
2002	0.18e
2003	0.21e
	Estimates

Qtrly EPS	+65%	+271%	+78%	+46%	+15%	+8%
	4QtrsAgo	3QtrsAgo	2QtrsAgo	LastQtr	NxtQtr	2QtrsOut

When to Hold

The bull market started in March 2003, exactly when URBN started to run. The P/E got to where it should be, and profits continued to grow, causing a four-fold gain in a year.

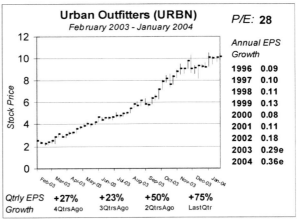

Urban Outfitters (URBN)	P/E: 28
February 2003 - January 2004	

Annual EPS Growth	
1996	0.09
1997	0.10
1998	0.11
1999	0.13
2000	0.08
2001	0.11
2002	0.18
2003	0.29e
2004	0.36e

Qtrly EPS Growth	+27%	+23%	+50%	+75%
	4QtrsAgo	3QtrsAgo	2QtrsAgo	LastQtr

When to Hold

In June 2004, I wrote about URBN, but still didn't buy it, and thought it was overvalued at 29 times profits. URBN doubled again in the next year and a half.

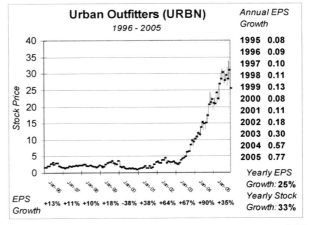

Urban Outfitters (URBN)	Annual EPS Growth
1996 - 2005	

1995	0.08
1996	0.09
1997	0.10
1998	0.11
1999	0.13
2000	0.08
2001	0.11
2002	0.18
2003	0.30
2004	0.57
2005	0.77

Yearly EPS Growth: 25%
Yearly Stock Growth: 33%

EPS Growth	+13%	+11%	+10%	+18%	-38%	+38%	+64%	+67%	+90%	+35%

Wholesale Sell

Wholesale Sell is a term I use when an investor is dissatisfied with his or her portfolio and dumps the entire thing all at once, regardless of price.

Doing a Wholesale Sell is like coming home and deciding to sell your car, home, furniture, clothing, electronics, and jewelry, just so you don't have to worry about it. You call people over and tell them you'll take whatever they'll give for your stuff. Those people you call over are complete strangers, people you'll never even meet – that's a Wholesale Sell.

When you sell all your stocks in one day to take whatever you can get, it is an emotional catastrophe. You know it's not logical, because *had* it been a logical and prudent decision, you would have at least sold at reasonable prices. Wholesale Sells often mark the bottom of a bear market. It's like the market was waiting for this investor to throw in the towel – then it goes up. I think every time someone Wholesale Sells, it sets them back a decade or more. Sometimes, they are so traumatized that they never invest in stocks again.

When you dump a whole portfolio of stocks that don't fit the mold, it's considered a cleansing, but not a Wholesale Sell. If you sell a bunch of stocks that need to be sold, salute. Congratulations on your new venture. Glad you see the light.

Watch Out For the Whiners

If you associate with a whiner, beware, for this person can pull you over to the dark side. Whiners always complain about the market, and they rarely blame themselves for their mistakes. They don't learn what the market tells them, and are always eager to tout their unproven, unsuccessful concepts.

If you start doing well in stocks, your whiner loved-one might convince you to Wholesale Sell and try another strategy— because his strategy wasn't working. The reason his didn't work out is because he isn't a winner, plain and simple. When whiners hurt their friends and family, they are some of the lowest forms of people.

In the tables to the right are the top five stocks in the Barron's 500 from 2003 to 2005. My clients owned twelve of the fifteen positions at the time, but owning some of the best stocks in the market didn't stop people from making the Wholesale Sell. Why did they sell? The top two reasons were that they hadn't made any money in the short term, and the market shook them out of everything.

Before doing the Wholesale Sell, look at the best company in the portfolio. Is the company setting new profit records almost every year? Check the ten-year charts on each stock. Is it still pointing up? If the answer is yes, then maybe you should hang on to this one.

2003 Barron's 500

Rank	Company	Symbol
1.	Coventry Healthcare	CVH
2.	Amgen	AMGN
3.	Advance PCS	ADVP
4.	Progressive	PGR
5.	Affiliated Comp Svcs	ACS
* Portfolio holdings notated in bold		

2004 Barron's 500

Rank	Company	Symbol
1.	Boston Scientific	BSX
2.	Countrywide Financial	CFC
3.	L-3 Communications	LLL
4.	D.R. Horton	DHI
5.	Omnicare	OCR
* Portfolio holdings notated in bold		

2005 Barron's 500

Rank	Company	Symbol
1.	United Health	UNH
2.	Caremark RX	CMX
3.	Coventry Healthcare	CVH
4.	Wellpoint	WLP
5.	Hovnanian Entrprs	HOV
* Portfolio holdings notated in bold		

Once you decide to hold on, it gets easier, and you start looking noticing other good stocks. If you walk through each stock, one by one, you may be amazed at what you might find.

Chapter U
When to Hold Stocks that No Longer Fit the Mold

No newsletter written

You will occasionally run into a situation when a stock no longer fits the mold, but you feel that the stock has great potential and you should hold onto it anyway. This often happens after a company missed earnings expectations, got hammered, and dropped to the lowest point of the year.

Holding stocks that don't fit the mold is a gray area. The reason this system works is because we take a step back and basically only have to know green numbers are good and red number are bad. If you have lots of red, the stock obviously doesn't fit the mold, which means we should sell and move on, right?

Wrong. Sometimes, common sense has to step in and keep us from doing something stupid. Say, I buy a stock at $30 and it gets hammered down to $15 on some bad news. If I sell here, the next stock would have to double to make up this loss. I'm not afraid of taking losses, especially in a diversified portfolio, but I get sick when I sell a stock and move the money into something else, only to see the sold stock return to previous highs. Argggggghhhh.

So many people follow the system in this book in one way or another, that when a stock goes from fitting the mold to no longer fitting the mold, the line to sell the stock is as long as the line at Wal-Mart on the morning after Thanksgiving.

I used to just dump stocks when they no longer fit the mold, no matter what. Coldly cut 'em. I would see these discarded stocks bounce back after I sold, and think to myself, there has got to be an exception to the rule.

The following guidelines should be applied to a stock that no longer fits the mold:

Use Some Freakin' Common Sense

Throughout this book, we have tried to disassociate ourselves from bringing our emotions, or beliefs, into our investment decisions. That's why this chapter is the hardest to write, because it's not quantifiable.

Take a step back and assess the situation. Is this stock way, way undervalued? Are you a sucker who's selling when you should be buying?

If a stock is down too far, smart value money managers step in and buy it dirt cheap. They buy the stock and sit through the storm, patiently waiting for the stock to double. Eventually, the company fixes the problem, and profit growth returns. The value guys sell the stock back to us, because now it's a growth stock again, and they pocket the difference.

Here's where the businessman in you steps to the plate. Like Donald Trump looking at real estate, think of where this stock will be in a year or two.

Occasionally, you may want to hold a stock that no longer fits the mold, just because the price is too low and the rebound will be exponential. Thus, there is a time to hang on to stocks that don't fit the mold, and there are rules to follow when doing so. Make sure that the following apply:

The P/E is Just Too Low

The main reason to hold a stock that's beaten down and no longer fits the mold is that it's just too cheap. If the P/E is low, say 8 to 12, then a slight rebound in the profits next year could make a profound contribution to the stock price.

Let's say you bought a stock last year at $20 that was making $1 in profits that year. Now, after you've owned the stock a year, the company suddenly says profits will drop 25%. On the news, the stock opens up for trading the next day at $7.50, giving you no chance to get out.

Given this scenario, here's what you're looking at:

Inside the Numbers: The Stock You Are Losing Money With	Profits		P/E		Median Stock Price
Year you bought:	$1.00	x	20	=	$20
This Year (now)	0.75	x	10	=	7.5

I figured the P/E to be 10 now. You're sitting on dead money, because the stock probably won't rally until investors are convinced that the company can get back on track.

If I'm in this situation, here's what happens next: I sell at $7.50 and the stock gets back to $20 in a year,

Inside the Numbers: The Stock You Are Losing Money With	Profits		P/E		Median Stock Price
Year you bought:	$1.00	x	20	=	$20
This Year (now)	0.75	x	10	=	7.5
Next Year	1.00	x	20	=	20
The Year After Next	1.50	x	20	=	30

then hits $30 the year after next, a 300% gain from the point I sold. I have done this so many times.

In this hypothetical situation, you should have held.

The Stock You Are Holding Cannot be a Large Position

When I hold a stock that no longer fits the mold, the first thing I do is make sure it's not a big position in my portfolio. The stock should not be a Top Ten holding or occupy more than 5% of your total portfolio. Consider selling half; you can always buy the shares back if it turns up.

One of my tricks of the trade is having my losers be the smallest positions in the portfolio. Some of this is self-fulfilling. If you have $1,000 in two stocks, and one drops 50% while one rises 50%, the loser is now worth $500 and the winner is $1,500. The good stock is now three times as large as the bad stock. Now, if the loser keeps dropping, it doesn't matter too much, because it's such a small position. You can also buy more shares of the winner, expanding the range between the two stocks even more.

The Potential Rebound is Huge

Like in the earlier example, if you do hold, at least make sure it'll be worth your while. If you're going to hold this stock, it should have huge upside. If you sit on a dog for a year and it goes up 10%, it's a waste of your time.

The Problem Should be Short-Term

Stocks with long term issues can take years to rise from the ashes. When the Exxon Valdez oil spill occurred in 1989, it may have been thought of as long-term, but had we taken a step back and looked at the big picture, it was one spill. Had it been a difficult situation such as, "Oil eats through tankers — oil can't be transported any longer," then **Exxon (XOM)** would have had a long-term problem.

The Problem Should be Correctable

In 1982, when cyanide was found in Tylenol, the situation was correctable. **Johnson & Johnson (JNJ)** stock closed at $1.84 on Tuesday, September 28, 1982. The next day, the first of seven deaths caused by cyanide poison occurred in the Chicago area. On October 5th, J & J issued a nationwide recall of Tylenol, as JNJ closed at $1.52, losing 15% in the seven days after the murders started. In November, Johnson & Johnson started packaging Tylenol in triple-protected packaging. JNJ was $1.82 on the last day of November 1982, and closed the year at $1.95. Now, in November 2006, the stock is in the $60s.

I Should Have Held Best Buy (BBY)

Chart One is a one-year view of **Best Buy (BBY)** from October 2001 to September 2002. Best Buy was a holding in my Growth Portfolio when it spiked down below $15 on a profit warning. The warning was bad. BBY not only warned but said profits would be lower than the year-ago period – negative profit growth. I sold BBY on the news. But notice on the right of Chart One BBY had a pretty good track record of growing profits each year. Also, the 2002 estimate showed only a slight decline in profits for the year. This stock was selling for only 12 times profits when I sold.

Chart Two is the next 12 months of Best Buy. I got out and the stock went up. In Chart Two quarterly profits were still worrisome, but the average of the four quarters was quite good. By May 2003, BBY had finished its 2002 calendar year, and managed to avoid the slight decline in annual profits after posting 20% profit growth in the May quarter. Consistency was intact, since profits did not fall on an annual basis.

Chart Three shows that the quarterly profit declines we saw earlier are not visible in the long term view of the stock. Instead, the sucker that sold at the very bottom is revealed.

The earnings table to the right shows the best point to buy BBY was in 1997 as profits jumped to $0.23 from nothing the year before. Had I bought then, I might have had the resolve to stick it out and hold Best Buy for the long term.

Inside the Numbers: BBY	Profits		P/E		Median Stock Price
1996	$0.00	x	N/A	=	$2
1997	0.23	x	13	=	3
1998	0.48	x	19	=	9
1999	0.72	x	35	=	25
2000	0.83	x	29	=	24
2001	1.18	x	19	=	23
2002	1.27	x	19	=	24
2003	1.63	x	18	=	29
2004	1.91	x	18	=	35
2005	2.27	x	19	=	43

When to Hold

Here's where I sold BBY. Profits were down 20%, but that was just one quarter. With a P/E of 12 and a solid growth history, I should have held the stock.

When to Buy

I should have bought BBY back at the breakout point of $22 in May of 2003, since profit estimates rose from $1.31 to $1.43 during the past three months.

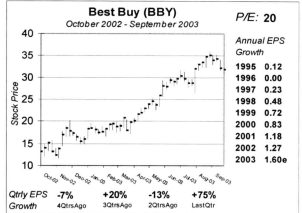

When to Hold

We should have bought Best Buy back in 1997, as the breakout price was $3 a share. From there, BBY would go on to rise another 1333% through 2005.

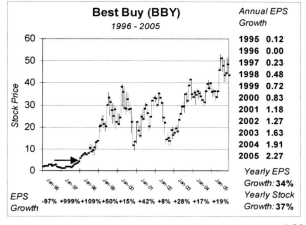

The Stock Should be One of Quality

Don't count on a dot-com to make a come-back. Make sure if you do hold, it's a solid stock, preferably a large cap with a solid record of certainty and consistency.

Wait No More Than One Year

Don't get caught in the game of, "Trust us, we'll turn things around next year," and hear the same story next year. Resilient stocks might have one down-year, as great companies have strong management that would push the stock back up to new heights. If it looks like two down-years, cut the loss and move on.

A Rally After Earnings is a Hopeful Sign

A good time to buy back is when the stock rally after earnings are announced. The rally is caused by institutions (big money) thinking the fears are relieved, and the stock is worth more. The numbers will probably still look bad at this point, but the stock might be turning the corner.

If You Do Sell, Buy the Stock Back If It Proves to Be Good

If you decide to part ways with the stock and move on (probably a good idea) you should buy the stock back on its rebound. Buying back a stock you have just sold for a loss can be difficult to swallow, which is why I usually hang on and ride the thing down. The results are sometimes good; often bad.

The ego is its toughest when considering buying back a stock we had lost money on. We try to argue against buying back the stock, and we often don't buy back because we are trying to "learn from our mistakes."

Don't Sit on Dead Money

If a stock of yours suddenly no longer fits the mold, it will often be dead money for a while. Dead money is money you have invested in something that doesn't grow, and doesn't even have a chance to grow.

Sitting on a former high-flyer that no longer fits the mold is sitting on Dead Money. Enough Dead Money stocks will choke the growth right out of your portfolio.

If you do decide to hang onto a stock that no longer fits the mold, do it only once in a blue moon. I may use this card once a year. The key with most of your investment decisions is to keep the emotions out of it, and to sell the stock when necessary.

Chapter V
Sell When Profits Slow or Fall

October 4, 2004

You should sell a stock when profit growth slows or when profits fall.

It sounds easy to me now. But during my first two years as an investor, I didn't know this. I thought if it were a good stock it would go up, if it was a bad stock it would go down. Then, I would sit on stocks that really didn't get me anywhere. It seemed like they didn't move for years. When bad news on one of my stocks came out, I would look for analyst opinions to see what they thought.

The first step in taking profits is to admit you're never going to get it perfect. Determine right from the start that you will either be wrong and sell a stock that keeps going up, or miss the top and give up a few dollars because you sold too late.

Sell When Profits Decelerate and the P/E is High

Sell when the P/E is high (30 or more) and when profit growth decelerates from rapid growth (+20%) to moderate growth (15-19%). At this point, the stock price can't keep up, and it has no upside potential.

To the right is a ten-year chart of **Bed, Bath and Beyond (BBBY)** from 1993 to 2002. This stock was a solid winner after going public in June 1992, compounding 43% a year through 2/01 (as profits grew 33% a year). I like the BBBY Annual Reports, because management includes financial data from every year the company was public.

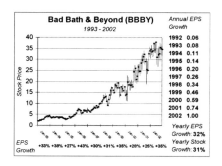

Above: *Bed, Bath & Beyond was a perfect stock in this chart (1993-2002) as it rose from $2 to $35.*

The 2002 – 2005 period wasn't so nice to BBBY stock, even though profits continued to chug along. The stock was flat-lined, because Wall Street expected Bed Bath & Beyond to reach a saturation point, thus the company wouldn't be able to expand at such a breathtaking pace.

Bad Bath & Beyond (BBBY) 1996 - 2005	Annual EPS Growth
	1995 0.14
	1996 0.20
	1997 0.26
	1998 0.34
	1999 0.45
	2000 0.59
	2001 0.74
	2002 1.00
	2003 1.31
	2004 1.65
	2005 1.92
EPS Growth +43% +30% +31% -28% +25% +35% +28% +25% +35% +26%	Yearly EPS Growth: 30% Yearly Stock Growth: 23%

Above: BBBY was relatively flat from 2003 through 2005 because profit growth slowed.

Notice in the table to the right that as profit growth declined from 31% in 2003 to 16% in 2005, the P/E also declined from 29 to 21. BBBY wasn't worth the big P/E anymore, because it wasn't growing profits fast.

Since the two factors in the equation (profits & P/E) went in opposite directions, the stock price was locked in a trading range. BBBY was unable to break out successfully and closed at $36 in 2005. It was $35 at the end of 2002.

Inside the Numbers: BBBY	Profits		P/E		Median Stock Price
2002	$1.00	X	32	=	$32
2003	1.31 (up 31%)	x	29	=	38
2004	1.65 (up 26%)	x	24	=	39
2005	1.92 (up 16%)	x	21	=	41

I first bought BBBY in July 2002 for $30 from my Growth Portfolio (which is geared for immediate gratification. I sold it from the Growth Portfolio at around $40 in January 2005, and held the stock in my Core Portfolio (long-term buy-and-hold stocks). In retrospect I should have sold all the shares. The P/E was just too high. The stock didn't go up.

A long-term shareholder with a low cost basis in BBBY could have held this stock, since the company was still growing profits each year at a decent, mid-teens rate.

Sell When Profits Stop Growing

If profits stop growing, the stock could come down due to a contracting P/E, as was the case with **Merck (MRK)** in 2001. The stock market recognized MRK's profit growth was coming to a halt in 2002, and felt a 24 P/E was too high. Consequently, the lower P/E multiplied by the same amount of profits yielded a lower stock price in 2002.

Inside the Numbers: MRK	Profits		P/E		Median Stock Price
2000	$2.90	x	26	=	$74
2001	3.14 (up 12%)	x	24	=	76
2002	3.14 (no growth)	x	17	=	52

Sell When Profits Decline

Schering-Plough (SGP) had a tougher time delivering profits than Merck and **Pfizer (PFE)** did. When SGP's profits declined in 2002, it created a double whammy, since P/E fell too. Thus, both factors in the equation were lower.

Inside the Numbers: SGP	Profits		P/E		Median Stock Price
2000	$1.64	x	27	=	$45
2001	1.58 (down 3%)	x	28	=	45
2002	1.34 (down 12%)	x	19		26

In the case of SGP, investors knew profits were going to slow a full year before the stock went through a major decline. Schering's top drug, Claritin, was coming off patent, and there wasn't anything in the pipeline that would make up for the lost profit.

Sell When Profits Are Expected to Slow or Fall

You must look ahead to expected slowdowns. Wall Street is always looking to the future when pricing stocks accordingly. If profits are expected to fall in the coming quarters, consider selling before the bad news is announced, especially if it's annual profit figures.

A Higher Tax Rate is Excusable

If you own a stock which has decelerating profit growth due to a higher tax rate, the rule Sell When Profits Fall may not apply. Wall Street sees that profits before taxes are still climbing, so the stock might not get punished. When profits fell 6% at **CareMark (CMX)** in 2003, the stock went from $16 to $25 because Wall Street knew this was due to a higher tax rate and the company was still growing.

Don't Sit on Dead Money

When you sit on a stock that has little chance of moving higher, you're sitting on Dead Money. After top winners have their profits peak, the stock can go through three to five years of dead money. Many investors, impressed with the stock's history, hold off on selling after the sell signals have been flashing. Other investors who have wanted to own the stock for years, and missed the gain in the first place, now buy the stock thinking it's cheap.

Microsoft (MSFT) from 2002 to 2005 was a perfect example of Dead Money. Few investors caught the big gains delivered to MSFT shareholders in the 1980s and 1990s because few bought the stock, thinking it was too high. So when Microsoft stock fell in 2001, investors got a lower stock price they wished for – and bought it.

Notice in the table to the right MSFT's P/E was 45 in 2000. Then as profit growth slowed to the single digits, the P/E came down, too. Slowing profit growth marked the top for Microsoft stock, forcing it into Dead Money status.

Inside the Numbers: MSFT	Profits		P/E		Median Stock Price
2000	$0.84	x	45	=	$39
2001	0.90 (up 3%)	x	32	=	30
2002	0.94 (up 2%)	x	30	=	28
2003	0.97 (up 2%)	x	25	=	26
2004	1.04 (up 4%)	x	21	=	26
2005	1.16 (up 6%)	x	22	=	26

When to Sell: Microsoft (MSFT)

Chart One shows MSFT as it peaked in March of 2000. After great stocks make long advances, the sell signal often occurs when the profit growth decelerates. On the right side of the chart, notice profits were expected to grow from $1.70 in 2000 to $1.90 in 2001. Expected profit growth of only 11% was Microsoft's first sell signal. Also, the stock was obviously not worth such a high valuation any more. So MSFT lost half its value, then went through years of back-and-forth stock moves when it went virtually nowhere.

Chart Two is MSFT during the following 12 months, just after the NASDAQ peaked. As quarterly profits slowed, money managers sold and small investors bought. When the big guys dump shares on the little guys, stocks go through wild price swings. This is the big guys dumping a bunch of shares, then waiting patiently for a better price to dump more.

Chart Three shows the stock during the ten-year period of 1996-2005. Chart One marked the top for MFT stock.

In 2004, Microsoft rewarded with a one-time $3 dividend, the largest dividend ever at the time. It was a waste of money. The news got Microsoft a lot of PR, and MSFT stock got a quick $3 boost. After the $32 billion was paid, the stock fell back down. Management should have used the

Inside the Numbers: MSFT	Profits		P/E		Median Stock Price
1996	$0.21	x	37	=	$7.87
1997	0.33	x	42	=	14
1998	0.45	x	58	=	26
1999	0.70	x	67	=	47
2000	0.86	x	45	=	39
2001	0.90	x	32	=	30
2002	0.94	x	30	=	28
2003	0.97	x	25	=	26
2004	1.04	x	21	=	26
2005	1.16	x	22	=	26

cash to purchase growing companies, and increase Microsoft's profits.

When to Sell

Comparing 2001's expected profits to 2000's yields 11% expected profit growth for next year. With a P/E of 62, Microsoft flashed sell signals.

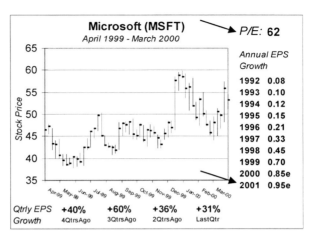

When to Sell

Notice quarterly profits at the bottom went from being up 23% to no-growth. Microsoft stock – even after this decline – was still overvalued with a P/E of 31.

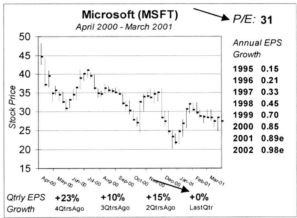

When to Sell

Note Microsoft grew profits rapidly in the 1990s but had sluggish growth during this decade. MSFT should have been sold when profits slowed.

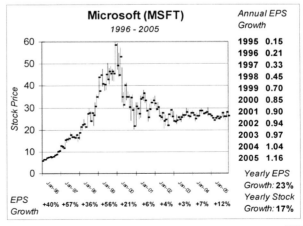

The Hot and Fresh Krispy Kreme

Krispy Kreme (KKD) made its first doughnuts in 1937, and after opening its first Manhattan store in 1996, still had less than 100 stores in operation. When the company went public in 2000, the stock market (and hungry customers

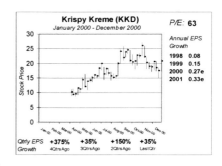

Above: Krispy Kreme in 2000. Although the 63 P/E seems high, KKD was trouncing estimates at the time.

across the U.S.) couldn't get enough Hot Original Glazed as lines at new locations went out the door for days or even weeks.

During the company's first 12 months of trading as a public company, Krispy Kreme's stock rose from $7 to $44. It makes me hungry just thinking about it. KKD kept blowing away estimates. 2001's profit growth was supposed to be 25%, but was 57% instead. This stock was hot.

Above: During this time KKD split 2-for-1 twice, so people who bought the stock the first week were up more than four-fold.

I bought Krispy Kreme for clients in the $40s, thinking, "People eat donuts." The purchase ended up being Dead Money at first, because I bought the stock when its P/E was high. But this was a stock market leader, and I didn't want to be left behind.

The year 2004 saw an abrupt end to KKD's fabulous run. Profit growth officially slowed on May 7, 2004, when the company said earnings would be $1.04 to $1.06 instead of the $1.17 we were expecting. This news sent the stock from $31 to $22 that day.

Why Krispy Kreme Fell

The table to the right is what I saw in KKD before the warning. Since the company was expected to grow profits 29% in 2004, I thought the stock

What KKD was worth before warning	Profits		P/E		Fair Value
2003	0.91				
2004	1.17e	x	29	=	$34

was worth 29 times earnings. 29 x 1.17 = $34, so with the stock selling at $32 at the time, it was pretty fairly valued.

After KKD lowered EPS estimates to $1.05, it lowered year-over-year growth to only 15%.

What KKD was worth after warning	Profits		P/E		Fair Value
2003	0.91				
2004	1.05e	x	15	=	$15

Companies that grow profits at 15% deserve P/Es of 15. 15 x 1.05 gives us a fair value of only $15.

With the stock trading in the low 20s, it was overvalued even after the drop, so I sold, and took a loss of 50%.

KKD Fried Investors

By the end of 2004, Krispy Kreme was looking to earn only $0.45, way down from previous estimates, but more importantly, lower than 2003.

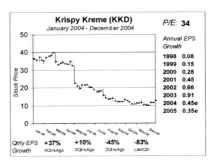

After hitting $40 earlier in 2004, the stock closed the year at $12, 70% off its high.

Above: *KKD during 2004 as profits went away.*

Krispy Kreme continued its downward spiral, hitting $4 in October 2005. Investors should have sold when profits slowed.

Chapter W
Sell When They Miss or Guide Lower
March 11, 2005

My first experience of owning stock in a company that missed earnings expectations was in 1997. My broker previously convinced me that the next big sector was going to be used-car-auto-finance. I agreed with his reasoning, and on February 10, 1997, we bought **General Acceptance Corporation (GACC)**, a finance company that worked with small used car lots like you see on the corner.

Then one day I got a call from my broker. He said he needed to show me some news. GACC came out with a press release, and he was going to fax it to me to read. I asked what it said, and his response was "Read it first."

I read the one-page piece, but I couldn't understand what it meant. I called my broker back and said, "What does this mean?" He said the company was going through some short-term difficulties, and he asked me what I wanted to do. Well, I didn't know what to do. He said the stock was down, but the situation looked correctable. I made the decision to stick with General Acceptance Corporation.

GACC fell hard the next day and continued to slide. I originally held out hope, then lost interest in the stock, and finally ignored it all together. I eventually sold GACC on October 21, 1998. My old tax returns show I invested $2121 in the stock, and when I sold, I received $138 back, for a loss of $1983. They might as well have taken the whole thing.

Sell When They Miss

When companies report quarterly profits, the figures are immediately compared to what the Wall Street analyst thought the company was going to make. If the reported numbers are less than the expected numbers, then the company missed Wall Street expectations, or missed the street.

An earnings miss is often the worst news for a stockholder. Earnings usually come out after the market closes or before it opens. When a miss occurs, the stock is usually down immediately, there's no chance to get out, since the bad news is public. Everybody knows the stock is worth less.

Missing estimates, if more than by a penny or two, is often a sell signal.

Sell When They Lower Guidance

When a company lets analysts know profits won't come in as good as anticipated before earnings are released, then management is lowering guidance or lowering expectations. Sometimes the analysts see a change for the worse in the company's business and lower the estimates themselves. Either way, it's called lowering the guidance.

Lowered guidance is also a sell signal. Pay close attention to yearly profit estimates after a company announces earnings. Sometimes, the company will hit the mark or beat the street, but lower annual expectations. Take the annual estimates more seriously. Lowering profit estimates is a bad sign, because it could be the first of many.

When a company either misses the street or lowers guidance, you don't have to sell the very day the bad news strikes. At the time, there is probably a flood of sellers, all trying to get out at once, so the stock might dip more than it should. I sometimes wait a day or two and sell if the stock rebounds a bit. Occasionally, I even wait a week or two for a better stock to put the proceeds into.

Lucent Missed the Street

On January 6, 2000, **Lucent (LU)** opened for trading at $73. Lucent's management then issued a first quarter 2000 press release stating, "The company expects earnings-per-share for last quarter to be in the range of 36 to 39 cents compared to 48 cents for the year-ago period."[6] Lucent was going to miss expectations, and have profits down as well: two sell signals. The stock swooned sharply lower, and closed the day at $52. Management still expected fiscal 2000s profits to be up 20% to 25% for the year.

Lucent wasn't just any other stock; it was the most popular stock to own. Originally a part of AT&T, this company was one of the world's leading developers of telecommunications equipment. Since its IPO in April, 1996, the stock had split two-for-one, twice. It rose from $8 to $75 in the 1990s. Younger people could relate to the Lucent story because they knew the fiber optic and networking was hot and experienced investors felt comfortable with AT&T.

Beware of the Opinions of Others

When a miss occurs, an investor often finds himself scrambling for news to help him figure out what to do. We surf the net, listen to conference calls, and accept analyst opinions on whether the stock will bounce back. Beware of the opinions of others. Management will often try to sugarcoat the situation and say that the best is yet to come. These may bring false hopes. Although analysts follow the company closely, sometimes they are too close to the situation to see clearly. Plus, what they say may not apply to your portfolio, in which only the best stocks reside.

Tiny Clues

Once a company starts lowering expectations, look for Tiny Clues clearing a path to another miss. Lucent got back on the road to profitability on April 20, 2000, as it grew second quarter profits 19%. Management claimed it had regained momentum this quarter and now estimated a profit growth of 17% in 2000. Notice this is lower than the

---

[6] from Lucent's press release *Lucent Technologies comments on expectations for first quarter 2000 earnings*, January 06, 2000.

20% to 25% growth for 2000 stated earlier — so essentially this is a small clue that Lucent will miss expectations for the year, a second time.

By now Lucent's stock was in a trading range, so there was no longer urgency to sell. LU was usually between $50 and $70 a share during the spring of 2000 — it actually got back over $70 for a little while in March. To owners of Lucent stock, it seemed like they were out of the woods.

Don't Let 'em Confuse You

The more confusing the numbers, the more leery you should be of the company, since they may have something to hide. Trouble arises when companies have "extraordinary charges."

July 20, 2000 -- Lucent lost $0.09 per share ($301 million) in the third quarter of 2000, but the top line of its press release said that pro forma EPS rose 30%. LU had charges of "$863 million for purchased in-process research and development related to recent acquisitions, $118 million amortization of goodwill and acquired technology, and a $287 million net loss from discontinued operations." Also, "We see our way to 20 percent top line and bottom line growth for fiscal 2001."[7] (Notice this is now 2001 not 2000). Whew! Sounds positive, though, right?

If you owned LU, you didn't read the press releases, you just knew the stock would bounce back. It did last time. Meanwhile, back at the ranch, Lucent just had a loss, missed the street, lowered estimates, broke through $50 on the downside, and was on its way to $20 by October.

The public was largely unaware to sell, having no formal education on earnings releases. Some depended on brokers for advice, some did the research on their own. Many held on, as if you would to a tree as a tornado hit – you just hang on, close you eyes, and hope for the best.

---

[7] from Lucent's press release *Lucent Technologies reports third fiscal quarter results*, July 20, 2000.

Lucent (LU)

During 2000, LU was one of the most widely-owned stocks in America. But even as the company continued to miss earnings estimates, I still couldn't get people to sell their stock. They just wouldn't do it.

Lucent's first sell signal was when the company warned in the first quarter (-11%) in **Chart One**. Profits bounced back in the second quarter (+19%), but that was all she wrote. The N/As at the bottom of the chart stand for losses. Still, even after the stock went all the way down to $11, the P/E was 29; really high for a company that was losing money. **Chart Two** just looks sick.

Lucent was one of the most difficult stocks to look up historical data on. The annual reports are flooded with extraordinary charges, many hundreds of millions of dollars of extraordinary charges and many different earnings per share numbers. **JDS Uniphase (JDSU)** was the same way, with annual reports of 100 pages or more. The more complicated an annual report is, the more skeptical you should be. It is easy to shove your dirty clothes under the bed when there is a big skirt there to cover it up.

Chart Three is a ten-year chart of LU, 1996 through 2005.

In late 2006, Lucent was acquired by France's Alcatel. The new stock symbol became ALU, with headquarters in Paris.

Inside the Numbers: LU	Profits		P/E		Median Stock Price
1996	$0.41	x	25	=	$10
1997	0.59	x	29	=	17
1998	0.87	x	42	=	36
1999	1.22	x	54	=	66
2000	0.93	x	48	=	45
2001	-1.38	x	N/A	=	13
2002	-1.23	x	N/A	=	4
2003	-0.29	x	N/A	=	2
2004	0.14	x	28	=	4
2005	0.17	x	18	=	3

When to Sell

Lucent's first sell signal was in April 2000 when it warned profits would drop 11%. The second was when LU broke out below $50, breaking out the wrong way.

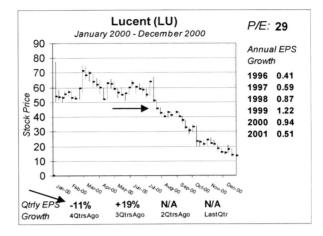

When to Sell

In 2001 LU got bumped up in January (why, I don't know). Even though the stock is way off its highs, there's still nothing positive here. Sell.

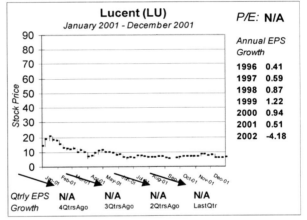

When to Sell

LU went on to lose money in 2001, 2002 and 2003, and traveled through Twosville on its way to $1 a share.

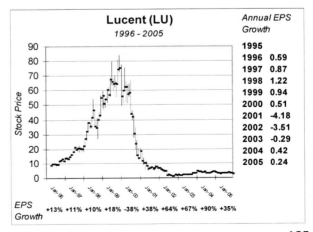

Promises, Promises

October 23, 2000 -- With the stock at $22, the company replaced its CEO and said it would now only break even for the fourth quarter of 2000, but explained, "It expects sequential improvement in results from operations each quarter for the rest of the fiscal year (2001)."[8]

Now LU has dropped from the $70s to the low $20s. People were convinced the stock would come back. Some investors would call their brokers to see what to do, but many brokers were in trouble. They didn't want the clients to sell and have to explain a big loss. Many thought if they held the stock for two or three years, and avoided the headlines, it would come back. They thought, "This is just temporary pain. Don't think about it."

December 21, 2000 -- Lucent predicted a loss of $0.25 to $0.30 for the first quarter of 2001, but "Fiscal year 2001 will be a rebuilding year, a turnaround year for Lucent," said Lucent Technologies Chairman and CEO Henry Schacht.[9] One month later, when these results were officially announced, the company stated in fine print, "As expected, the company posts a pro forma loss from continuing operations of 30 cents per share,"[10] as if management was saying it met expectations, as if they were saying they were out of the weeds, since it was expected.

Lucent stock was now in the teens. Most investors who bought Lucent had now accumulated huge losses and thought it was now far too late to turn back. Like when I get lost driving, and need to stop for directions. Who, me? Stop for directions? Just a little longer, it's right up here...

---

[8] from Lucent's press release *Lucent Technologies Board of Directors names Henry Schacht Chairman and CEO,* October 23, 2000

[9] from Lucent's press release *Lucent Technologies reports results of operational and fiscal review,* December 21, 2000

[10] from Lucent's Press release *Lucent Technologies announces seven-point restructuring plan to reduce expenses by $2 billion and significantly improve cash flow,* January 24, 2001

I tried to show prospective clients they should sell their Lucent, but some would treat me as an enemy for saying such disparaging remarks. Denouncing the stock was as if I was passing judgment on one's child who had been arrested for a crime, but had yet to be tried. I would draw the picture out on a napkin for them, and tell them to think about it. This gave the investor time to call the other broker, who would say "it'll be back" and "long-term." Then, the investor would sit with the stock, and wait for the good news.

April 4, 2001 -- Good news. Lucent reported its second quarter 2001. The headline read, "Lucent Technologies reports sequential improvement for second fiscal quarter 2001 as pro forma loss per share from continuing operations improved 5 percent from a loss of 39 cents to a loss of 37 cents."[11] Could you imagine if I told my customers if I lost 39% of their portfolio one year, and 37% the next? "Congratulations. It's an improvement?"

In a separate press release sent out on the same day, the headline read, "Lucent technologies says rumors of bankruptcy are baseless." LU had now fallen to $6.75, and was on its way to Twosville.

Take Preventive Measures

Lucent's fall shook the nation, although the headlines don't reveal the true devastation caused. The stories were kept private and confidential. The real issue was that there was an emotional attachment to the stock. People wouldn't give up, leave, or let go. Lucent stock was one of the most popular stocks to own in 2000. It often burned and buried shareholders so bad they got out of owning stocks altogether. Still, the story makes an excellent case study, one we can learn from and teach our children, if we look at the Lucent debacle in a brighter light. Now we know how important it is to sell when stocks miss or guide lower.

---

[11] from Lucent's press release *Lucent Technologies reports sequential improvement for second fiscal quarter 2001*, April 24, 2001

Chapter X
Sell if the Stock is too Low

August 10, 2005

It is paramount to understand our attachment to the stocks we already own if we really want to stand among the elite stock investors. Once we know the rules for What to Buy, When to Buy and When to Sell, the main obstacle is following through on the plan ahead. Don't be an investor who cannot – will not — make the move to rid themselves of their losers. Admit the stock is a dog, and sell it.

We must be fully aware of the Emotional Cycle we go through when a stock rises and falls. Only then do we understand what we need to do to improve ourselves.

The Emotional Cycle of Owning a Stock

Fear. Step one occurs when a stock we never heard of breaks out to a new high. The company has great profit growth, but we are apprehensive of buying the stock since we are not familiar with it. Only trend-setters, people who have to own the newest electronic gadget, buy the stock here.

Enthusiasm. Now, the stock starts to move higher, setting new highs along the way. A few articles are written about the company's secret to success. But you're still not buying it. You like the stock, but something -- you don't know what it is – keeps you from buying.

Greed. By now, the great stock is scampering higher and higher, and you are envious of those who bought at lower levels. The company starts getting on magazine covers and getting plugged on TV, because money managers are saying, "It's a buy!" These bullish comments provide reinforcement to you that this is a stock to own. You are now more comfortable with the stock, since you are more familiar with it.

Greed steps in, and you can't stand the fact the stock keeps rising when you don't have any – so you buy.

Love. You now adore your new-found stock. You can't wait to come home and see what the stock closed at for the day, thinking things like "I'll never sell this stock" or "this is the best stock ever." But instead of going up, the stock is now making volatile swings, mostly down. Still, the emotional attachment makes you think the company can do no wrong. You tell your friends all about it, and even buy more yourself. You are feeling good about yourself, even though the stock is past its peak.

Denial. At this stage, the stock is falling, but the analysts still love the stock. Your broker may be more bullish on the company's prospects than ever before. You convince yourself, "It'll be back." You change your thinking to, "If it can get back to what I bought it for, I'll sell and get out at even." The stock continues to free-fall, but you refuse to sell and take the small loss, calling it a "long-term investment."

Ignorance. The once-great stock has now fallen dramatically, causing an embarrassing loss in your portfolio. The company starts to miss profit estimates. The stock chart looks bad. The sector is in turmoil. After ignoring the facts for months, or even years, you ignore the stock altogether. You stop reading your brokerage account statements and find other hobbies to pass the time. New stock market leaders begin to take off, but you are unaware of them because you haven't been doing your research. Unfortunately you have not truly given up emotionally, since you haven't sold your dog stock yet.

Anger. You are now disgusted that the stock continues to drop. Blame is placed on the broker, the analysts, and anyone but yourself. You start to believe that all CEO's are crooked and even start blaming the market, saying things like "you can't make money in stocks" and you look for alternative investments like real estate. You hate the stock, but still won't sell.

189

Sadness. The dog stock you bought at its highs has long since hit rock bottom, and stayed there. Your anger has subsided, and you are now regretful. You finally give up hope and sell, throwing in the towel. At this point, not only have you lost money on this laggard stock, but your failure to accept the truth has caused you more money in opportunity loss. You should have moved your money into other stocks that have since doubled, tripled, or even quadrupled in price.

Cisco was Different

The trick to beating the emotional trap discussed above is self-awareness. Be cognizant of the fact that emotions play a part in stock selection, then acknowledge that you will go through the phases above for yourself. Know your own weaknesses.

In 1999, the only stocks that fit the mold — or were even worth owning — were tech stocks. Old manufacturing stocks like **General Electric (GE)** had neither the profit growth nor the chart patterns of market leaders. Income stocks were dead in the water. Who needed a 6% yield when growth stocks can give 20% or more a year?

After the 1990s, there were a handful of growth stocks people stayed in love with, even after it was widely known that the company was no longer a stock market leader. In addition to **Lucent (LU)**, **America Online (AOL)**, **EMC (EMC)** and **Cisco Systems (CSCO)** were a few of the most widely-held stocks in the country and continued to be when they fell from grace. Investors didn't want to sell low.

It was easy to see it was time get out of Lucent and AOL, since profits were dwindling. Cisco Systems was different. Its profits kept jumping as the stock fell. It still fit the mold, so I held on. After riding Cisco up into $80s in March of 2000, the stock corrected with the market.

When, at $55, the company said inventories were getting high (a sign that things aren't being sold as fast as they should have) I ignored the sell signal.

By February of 2001, last quarter's profits were up 50%, and my estimates for the next two quarters were for growth of 35% and 23%. As Cisco fell further, it became more and more attractive to me. The company repeatedly said that business conditions were tough, Cisco always beat the street.

My love for Cisco was strong. It was my top stock and would be the one to survive. So I thought. Until the company warned of lower profits, and I was stuck, holding Cisco at $22 as it no longer fit the mold.

An Upside-down Saucer or Bowl

One clue that should have told me to sell is the chart pattern Cisco made on its way down. A one-year chart of Cisco in 2000 resembles the outline of an upside-down saucer or bowl, like the one of **Enron (ENE)** at the right. This chart pattern is

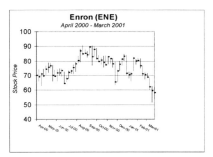

characteristic of a stock that's beginning a downward move. This chart kept me from buying Enron.

Sell After a Breakout to the Downside

Above: Enron made an upside down saucer, or bowl, pattern as it fell from its highs in 2001.

If the stock is selling at a 52-week low, you have a situation to evaluate. Did the stock just breakout to the downside? In Cisco's case, the stock seemed to stay above $50 until breaking below it in October 2000. I held and by the end of the week CSCO was back above $50. But this temporary lift only made me feel more at ease with the stock, so when Cisco fell below $50 again, I held steadfastly. When it broke through $40, I couldn't sell here.

Cisco Systems (CSCO) Fell Before Profits Did

If you have a stocks with an upside-down saucer chart pattern, take a deep breath, clear your mind, and try to get a big-picture view of the stock.

Chart One is a view of Cisco Systems during the 1990s. Cisco was one of the hottest stocks of the decade, especially at the end. This is what the ten-year view of what CSCO looked like at the end of 1999, with profits up every year (right) and profit growth very strong each year (bottom).

Chart Two is Cisco at the end of 2000. Here, the stock is falling, but all the numbers are still bullish (so I held on — then bought more). Notice also how quarterly profits (bottom) were still growing handily and the next two quarters look great. To me, the more Cisco went down, the more attractive it got.

Chart Three is the stock during 2001. After the January quarter was announced (the 50% profit growth bottom left), I had estimates that the next quarter's profits would be up 35%. Instead, Cisco had profits down 77%. Also, it was obvious that profits for the year would be down significantly. I thought to myself, "Now what do I do?" I was stuck.

What I did was, I took a step back and assessed the situation, keeping my emotions out of it. Let's face it, CSCO no longer fits the mold, since profits were declining, and this wasn't a one or two-quarter thing. Cisco had to be sold.

When Cisco fell from grace in 2000 and 2001, I was too focused on the stock's history and the aura surrounding the company. Had I taken a step back and looked at the big picture, I might have noticed that all technology was fighting an uphill battle – the sector was out of favor. Analyst estimates kept falling, but I was still convinced that CSCO would beat the street, as it had in the past. It didn't.

When to Hold

Cisco in the 1990s showed it could grow year-in, year-out. It was a leader. This chart, all the data, the returns – how perfect.

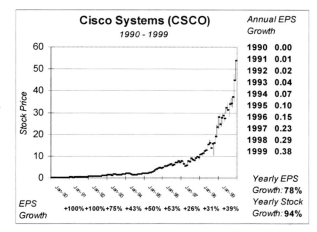

When to Sell

The breakout of the upside-down bowl pattern at $50 is a breakout to the downside, which is a clear sell signal in this chart. I saw it, but didn't listen.

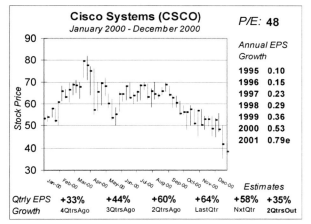

When to Sell

I ended up getting out at $22. In retrospect, this turned out to be the correct call, since Cisco hovered around $20 the next four and a half years.

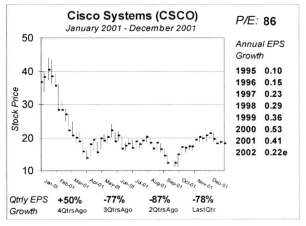

A Shift in the Market

Noticing huge market shifts will be paramount to your success. A market shift, in my opinion, is a shift between asset classes like Large Cap Growth (the stocks in this chapter), Large Cap Value (usually old blue chips that often pay dividends), Small Caps, International stocks, and real estate stocks (known as REITs).

The Herd

Picking up on a shift in the market and being able to adjust to the future winning group can lead you to drastically outperform The Herd. The Herd is the mass of people who often come late to the party, travel in a group, and are seldom right. They cling to others in The Herd for support, and often are two steps behind Smart Money, who use stock market history as a guide to their decision making.

In 1999 and 2000, The Herd ran ramped. Obsessed with the spectacular returns of the tech stocks, it plowed into techs, with little regard to risk. Since more people would push into stocks like Cisco, **Sun Microsystems (SUNW), Oracle (ORCL)**, EMC and **Nortel (NT)**, these stocks would rise due to supply and demand constraints.

Unfortunately, when the market shifted, and it was time to leave, The Herd was not skilled in technical analysis (reading a chart), and ignored fundamental sell signals. Smart Money, on the other hand, got out quicker, and fled to safety in another asset class.

Go Into the Forgotten Asset Class

When speculation occurs in a certain area in a way which Large Cap Growth in the late 1990s did, the Smart Money moves to an asset class which has been neglected all these years. The asset class to go into is often a forgotten one in which the stocks have not moved in years, and one which contains many stocks with low P/Es.

Chapter X – Sell When the Stock is Too Low

After Large Cap Growth peaked in 2000, Smart Money fled to Small Caps, which led the market through 2006, when this book was written. The first half of the 2000s was a period of low interest rates. Large Cap Value and REITs both paid dividends, and did well because they were sought out by people who needed income to live on. For five years, Large Cap Growth was filled with Dead Money.

Making this move into a better asset class is often a slow process for The Herd. Headlines and opinion dominate its thought process, backed up by statistical evidence from the past three-to-five years. Past performance does not imply future gain, which was never more evident when I spoke at a women's investment club in 2001. I spoke to the club a year or so earlier and mentioned **Alliance Gaming (ALLY),** before it went up five-fold (they didn't buy it), and suggested they move away from Large Cap Value into Large Cap Growth — especially technology.

Now, I was saying they should have a portion of the portfolio in REITs. They looked at me as if I had gone mad, since I was the one who told them to own more tech in the first place. To simplify the process of getting into REITS, I brought a REIT mutual prospectus. This idea was shot down, because REITS had done nothing the past three years. In the end, REITS would average greater than a 20% a year for the next four years, beating the market by a wide margin.

By 2006, REITs were high, and Large Cap Value was a top class. My Income Portfolio was up beyond expectations through October. It had been rising for years, and had just had a sudden spike up; these are clues which often preclude the end of a run. I knew it couldn't last, and looked like a market top in Large Cap Value. It seemed the market was about to shift back to growth.

Chapter Y
Sell When the Stock is Too High

No newsletter written

The stock market in 1999 couldn't have been better.

The late 1990s was a great time to be in stocks. 1995-1997 saw the large, blue chip companies rise (Large Cap Value). Then in 1998-1999, the market shifted as tech and telecom led the way (Large Cap Growth). Lots of mutual funds averaged more than 20% a year. 20% a year? That's what people expected – really. They did.

The Technology Bubble of the Late 1990s

In 1999, we said, "Things were different now." The Internet transformed how we do business, how we entertain ourselves, and how we get information. People were flocking online, and companies were more than happy to invest in getting positioned on the net.

Additionally, because computer systems and programs were expected not to work after the clock hit 12 on December 31, 1999. Some programs only kept two digits for the "year." There was a fear that the computers would break down on 1/1/2000, and our finances would disappear – no lie. So companies spent big bucks to fix their systems.

The combination of Y2K (year 2000) spending and Internet spending gave networking companies more business than they could handle. Since so many companies had to tackle the expenses of Y2K and the Internet at the same time, IT budgets exploded in 1999.

Concurrently, fiber optics was the new "plastic." Broadband had huge potential. The story was easy. In 1998-1999, most of us were using **America Online (AOL)** for internet access. AOL was slow, often taking five minutes to load a page. Sometimes, you just sat there, as the blank screen tried to load. Fiber optics would allow more data to travel at faster rates, so telecom companies were eager to spend billions to lay fiber optic cables underground and in the sea. **Corning's (GLW)** CEO was asked how long this spending spree on fiber would continue, assuming the answer would be "years." Instead, he answered, "In generations."

In 1999 the only stocks which fit the mold were tech stocks. The big blue chips had sluggish profit growth, and their stocks weren't doing anything. So Technology was the place to be.

Yahoo! (YHOO), eBay (EBAY) and a handful of other Internet companies were starting to make profits and pave a new frontier —a limitless one. Others stocks had no more than a dream. But the market was thirsty for new companies that were capable of the next big thing. Most of these new companies lost money, and still their stocks soared higher.

"I Just Want to Own Tech"

Tech mutual funds were averaging 35% a year. As Investors saw the great track records of tech funds, they put more money into the funds. Mutual fund managers would take the new money and buy more tech stocks, like **Global Crossing (GBLX)** and **CMGI (CMGI)**, sending the tech stocks even higher.

The online trading revolution also brought more money into stocks. People were convinced that they could manage their portfolios on their own and make more in their pajamas than at work.

People who were normally afraid of stocks were now enthusiastic about investing in them. They got greedy about the gains that were being made, and they continued to shift more assets to the aggressive part of the stock market.

Speculation in the Market

In 1999-2000, an incredible amount of speculative capital flowed into small companies with promising futures. Some companies possessed rapidly growing earnings, others did not. All rose exponentially.

> *As the long bull market was reaching its final peak in 1969 another mistake occurred. To understand what happened it is necessary to recreate the psychological fever which gripped most investors in technological and scientific stocks at the time. Shares of these companies, particularly many of the smaller ones, had enjoyed advances far greater than the market as a whole. During 1968 and 1969 only one's imagination seemed to cap the dreams of imminent success for many of these companies. Some of these situations did have genuine potential, of course. Discrimination was at a low ebb. For example, any company serving the computer industry in any way promised a future, many believed, that was almost limitless.[12]*

As Confidence Was Highest, the Market Had a Free-fall

The end started out as "buy on a dip." What an opportunity to get these great stocks for 20% to 30% off. Buyers thought, "Soon, the stocks would bounce right back to their old highs." When they dropped 30% again, it looked so easy to trade the volatility. The Man said that if you watched closely, you would see that the highs get lower, and the lows get lower as well. OK with me. I'm smart, I can do it.

But I couldn't. Soon, it was a free fall. Gosh, if it would just get back close enough. I wish I could go back. What a nightmare. The dead pain in your gut. Walking around like a zombie, trying to fit in with the others. But the others were going through the same thing. It seemed like everyone was making so much money, but it was just a facade. I

---

[12] *From Common Stocks and Uncommon Profits*, Philip A Fisher, pgs 231-232,1996 John Wiley & Sons.

would cry when I left in the morning, then once at work just stare at the screen. I got used to the pain. The stocks would be flat one day and up the next, creating euphoria, then the third, fourth, fifth—down, down, down. Like having your presents stolen from under the tree.

History Repeats Itself in the Stock Market

This kind of speculative run-up in the market usually occurs every 30 years or so.

> *In the first place, and on this very point, nearly all these brilliant performers were young men—in their thirties and forties—whose direct financial experience was limited to the all but continuous bull market of 1948-1968. Secondly they often acted as if the definition of a "sound investment" was a stock that was likely to have a good rise in the market in the next few months. This led to large commitments in newer ventures at prices completely disproportionate to their assets or recorded earnings.*
>
> *This period saw a complete debacle in a host of newly launched common stocks of small enterprises—the so called hot-issues—which had been offered to the public at ridiculously high prices and then had been pushed up by needless speculation to levels little short of insane. Many of these lost 90 percent and more of the quotations in just a few months.[13]*

I believe the market peaked in March 2000, because that was when the first quarter of 2000 ended. Any company that needed to spend on Technology had their projects done in 1999, and by 2000, it didn't need anything else. When it was obvious that technology revenue would be horrible, the bubble burst.

Fortunately, there is a way for us to see when the risk in a stock is blisteringly high. The stock's chart shows clues that tell you to sell.

---

[13] *From The Intelligent Investor*, Benjamin Graham, 1973, Harper Collins Publishers, pg 34. This paragraph was in reference to the 1962 speculative top.

Qualcomm (QCOM)

Qualcomm invented DMA or Code Division Multiple Access. Among CDMA's advantages, multiple signals can share a single channel, so radio frequencies can handle many calls simultaneously. That gives us better voice quality and fewer dropped calls as we move from one coverage area to another. Qualcomm licenses CDMA to telecom manufacturers, getting money by charging an up-front fee and a monthly fee (recurring revenue). So every time you pay your cell phone bill, Qualcomm gets a slice. QCOM became the best stock of 1999 because the growth opportunity looked limitless.

Chart One is Qualcomm's 1998 chart – very positive. The only negative is the -35% profit growth two quarters ago. The P/E is calculated on 1998 earnings. I didn't have QCOM on my radar, so I did not retain 1999 estimates. I'm guessing the P/E was around 30 at the time, as profits just grew 61%.

Chart Two is QCOM during 1999. In March 1999, QCOM broke out to new highs. By April, earnings were released and expectations for the year elevated. In May, with the stock at over $200 a share, Qualcomm split two-for-one. Still, QCOM raced higher, and was back over $200 by October. Analysts kept upping price targets, with the most infamous target at $800. In November and December, the stock chart turned up almost like a rocket, opening November at $221 a share, hitting a high of $740, before splitting four-for-one late in 1999.

Chart Three is QCOM in 2000, digesting its gains from 1999. After the uncomfortable decline, Qualcomm was still up more than ten-fold in two years.

Inside the Numbers: QCOM	EPS		P/E		Median Stock Price
1998	$0.09	x	27	=	$3
1999	0.15	x	160	=	48
2000	0.42	x	110	=	57

What to Buy

QCOM bases during 1998. Note profits were up 61% last quarter. A move past this $4 high would be a breakout and a buy signal.

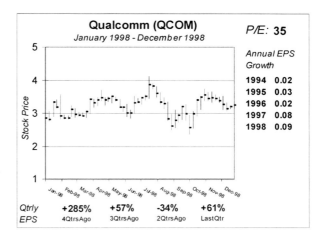

When to Buy

Qualcomm was the top stock of 1999, gaining 2587%. But looking at the chart, the stock was too high – as was the 180 P/E.

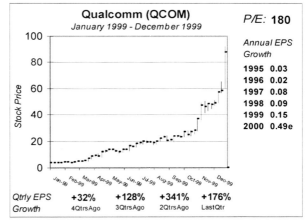

When to Sell

The inability to grow profits the last two quarters was a significant factor in the Qualcomm's fall from grace in 2000.

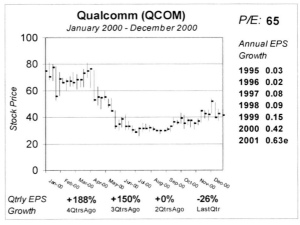

One reason QCOM raced higher at the end of 1999 was that everybody had to own the stock, so they bought it by the bushels. Qualcomm was all hyped-up. Mutual fund managers loaded the boat. The managers felt they had to show investors they owned the stock at year-end, as top holdings would show up in the fund prospectus.

Five Clues a Stock is in a Speculative Run-up

Fortunately, there are hints that the fantastic stock you own might be due for a fall. Here's five warning signs to look for.

1. After going up most of the year, the stock suddenly doubles or triples within a few months. Maybe the stock is now jumping $10 a day, or one day, it opens up at a price much higher than it's ever been (this is called a gap up). A top may be here. Imagine you're climbing a mountain. The first leg of the trip, you are walking uphill. The second leg is steeper; you're hiking heavier terrain. The third leg is almost straight up; you climb it with ropes, harnesses and tools used to climb walls of rock. If your stock chart looks like this mountain, consider selling. Stocks fall the way we might fall during our hiking trip. Fall on a hill, no big deal. Fall off a cliff and you drop hard to the next flat landing, which may be far, far below.

2. The stock is very volatile, with wild price swings — down big one day, up big the next. Down days could be mutual fund managers dumping huge amounts of the stock onto the market. As the managers wait patiently for some time, the stock rises, and then the managers dump more. More often than not, the fund managers know something you don't — that it's time to get out.

3. The stock's P/E is greater than 50. If, next year, the P/E comes down to a more-reasonable 25, then profits have to at least double in the next year, just to have the stock where it is today. Lots of downside but not much upside.

4. Hype Will Only Help. The fun part about owning stocks with catalysts is they have a chance of becoming the talk of the town and racing higher in a short period like QCOM did. When everybody is talking about this stock – all piling in at once – the stock is all hyped up. If a chart pattern like the one of QCOM 1999 develops, its time to leave. If you think the run will continue, sell half and play both sides of the fence.

5. People who don't know stocks start telling you to buy this one. The news is already out, with every Joe Schmoe buying into the story. Think about it: Who else is there to buy the stock if everybody owns it now?

Stocks that have speculative run-ups often show excellent profit growth as they peak in price, so selling high is tougher than it looks. The stock may be showing triple-digit profit growth after the peak, and continues this superior profit growth quarters into the future. Still, the stock peaked ahead of time. Never underestimate the market's intelligence. It wrote the book we all try to grasp.

If you do miss the top, which is likely, at least get out after the stock has started to fall. During the fall, you will be convinced the stock will rise again, so keep looking at the chart and try to make a rational decision. Like in the climbing example above, the next stop is a long way down. To estimate (guess) where the stock will fall to, look for the last price the stock broke out at.

The way to spot a speculative stock as it is topping is to first make yourself aware of what past chart-toppers looked like. Learn the traits and consider selling because the stock is too high.

Chapter Z
Sell When the Market is High

January 7, 2005

This is when you learn how to sell at the top of the market.

The toughest thing about owning stocks is when to sell. Sell a big winner early, and you're the sucker. It's incredibly difficult to trade your way to the top, so most of us need to buy and hold, hope to hit a home run, and wish for the best. Inside, we winners crave more than just 12%.

So you follow a system that allows you to find tomorrow's winners today. Your stocks do just as you thought they would. Everything is going right. But when do you sell a good stock, one that still fits the mold, after a big gain?

Only Sell a Portion of Your Good Stock

The best answer to When to Sell may be to play both sides of the fence. Why not sell some of your big winner and continue to hold some as well? This way, you're able to knock down some profits and use the proceeds to invest in hopefully the next Home Run, while also owning some shares if the stock keeps rising. Selling some of your top performers when they're high gives you an opportunity to buy more if the stock takes a big dip. The biggest downside is, if the stock keeps rising at an alarming rate, you will look back and say to yourself, "I should have held the whole thing."

Take Profits When the P/E is Much Higher Than the Company's Profit Growth Rate

When a stock's P/E gets abnormally high, it may be time to start selling some of your holdings. A good rule of thumb is to sell when the P/E is two to three times the profit growth, expected profit growth in the next two quarters, or estimated profit growth over the long-term. For example, the peak in **Wal-Mart (WMT)** came in December 2000 at $70, the company was selling for 50 times earnings and profits were growing 21%. Fifty times profits, in retrospect, was clearly high for a firm that grew profits at 21%.

Even though WMT was a long-term leader, it's been a laggard since 1999, because the stock got ahead of itself; through the combination of a bull market and higher-than-normal profit growth in 1999. In 1999, WMT was expected to grow in the future at 17% a year but grew 29% that year. What a bull market actually does is give stocks a higher multiple, or P/E, than stocks

Inside the Numbers: WMT	EPS		P/E		Median Stock Price
1997	$0.78	x	21	=	$16
1998	0.99	x	30	=	30
1999	**1.28**	**x**	**42**	**=**	**54**
2000	1.40	x	39	=	55
2001	1.50	x	33	=	50
2002	1.81	x	30	=	54
2003	2.03	x	26	=	53
2004	2.41	x	23	=	56
2005	2.63	x	18	=	48
2006	2.92e	x	15	=	45

should have. Note in the table above that WMT's P/E jumped in 1999. The combination of 29% profit growth and an excited stock market pushed WMT stock much higher than warranted — in this case, to 42 times earnings. There was little chance that the big Wal-Mart could continue 20% plus profit growth. In my opinions the stock was way too high, so I stayed away.

When stocks have P/Es that are truly too high, two outcomes can occur. First, a stock could buckle through a quick correction, either on its own or with other stocks in a bear market. Bear markets deflate P/Es all-around. The second outcome is that the stock could go back and forth for years while the earnings catch up. 15% growers are worth 15 times earnings. So between 2000 and 2006, the Wal-Mart stock merely treaded water, while company profits kept growing. Slowly, the P/E shrank, until the stock was selling for what it should have in the first place: 15 times earnings, which WMT hit in 2006.

The Great Home Depot

One stock that burned investors in the early 21st century – after it was one of the great stock market winners of our time – is **Home Depot (HD)**. Home Depot opened its first stores in the Atlanta market in June 1979. From the get-go, Home Depot smashed all sales and profit projections. On September 22, 1981, the company had its initial public offering on the NASDAQ under the symbol HOMD.

One of the first signals that told investors Home Depot was a great stock was in 1982 in its first annual report as a public company. The company stated sales increased 131% as profits expanded 168%. A smart investor could have seen this stock as a "buy" and picked up shares of Home Depot in the early 1980s — or at least put the stock on the radar.

1983 had even more buy signals with profits up each quarter at rates of 50%, 63%, 550%, and 117% respectively.

Unfortunately, 1985 brought a sell signal—a down year in profits. The company made an acquisition mistake by buying a similar company called Bowater Home Centers, which was in the markets that Home Depot was not, such as Mobile, Dallas and Baton Rouge. Bowater Home Centers was a bad investment, as it had shoddy goods and poor customer service. Consequentially, profits declined in 1985.

Historically, 1986 proved to be the time to get on the Home Depot express, because profits rebounded past the old record high as the stock's P/E was 18 or so.

The year 2000 was clearly a year to take profits in Home Depot, since the P/E was a lofty 47 as profits grew only 10%. If you had owned HD for a long time and had big gains, you could've sold some shares and kept some, since Home Depot did not break our cardinal rule of declining profits. You could have also sold the whole position, depending on your investment style.

How to Spot a Market Top

The 2000 market top, and subsequent decline, had vast similarities to the stock market in the early 1970s. Big market declines often occur once in a generation. Those who get burned often swear off stocks for good and place blame on the market, instead of taking the time to analyze the situation and realize it was their stocks that created the uncomfortable situation. The next generation will not be aware of the sell signals which flash at the top of the market, unless you teach them.

When a top is occurs speculation bulldozes over rationale. Greed trumps risk. People buy high, as we saw with the QCOM example.

During the late 1990s, Large Cap Growth stocks had great returns as many stocks rose 35% a year. The market topped in 2000, when Large Cap Growth stocks were overpriced. When I say of overpriced, I mean the P/Es were large. Growth stocks also had great gains from the late '60s through December 1972, and then crashed in 1973-1974. Perhaps the best synopsis of the growth stocks of 1972 was done by Jeremy Siegel in *Stocks for the Long Run*.

> *The "nifty fifty," as these stocks were called, was a group of premier growth stocks, such as Xerox, IBM Polaroid, and Coca-Cola that became institutional darlings in the early '70s. Many investors did not seem to find 45, 50 or even 60 times earnings at all an unreasonable price to pay for the world's preeminent growth companies, although many of these stocks sold for barely half that price just a few years earlier.*

In retrospect, the 2000 market top was vastly similar to the one that occurred one generation earlier. In both instances, the time to sell was when investors got enamored with the top stocks, and ran them higher until the P/Es were two to three times higher than the companies were expected to grow.

When to Sell: Home Depot (HD)

Chart One shows HD at the market top in March 2000. The stock's P/E was 52 while next quarter's profits were expected to grow 29%. 52 times earnings was expensive for Home Depot at the time, because the already company seemed to have a store in every up-and-coming neighborhood. All that was left were the undesirable locations so **growth opportunity** wasn't there for HD to continue 25% growth.

In **Chart Two** we see Home Depot in January 2003. Amazingly, in less than three years later, HD had gone from extremely high to absurdly low. In the Inside the Numbers table to the right, note that 2003 was the year HD had its lowest P/E.

Chart Three is Home Depot from 1995 to 2004, with the annual profit growth rates plotted along the bottom. Notice on the right that profits are up each year, which means no true sell signal occurred for long-term shareholders. Long-term winners such as Home Depot can usually be held through tough times as long as profits keep rising.

Inside the Numbers: HD	EPS		P/E		Median Stock Price
1981	$0.002	x	20	=	$0.04
1982	0.005	x	36	=	0.18
1983	0.009	x	56	=	0.50
1984	0.013	x	34	=	0.44
1985	0.007	x	49	=	0.34
1986	0.020	x	18	=	0.35
1987	0.037	x	18	=	0.66
1988	0.05	x	16	=	0.81
1989	0.07	x	20	=	1.42
1990	0.10	x	25	=	2.46
1991	0.13	x	38	=	5
1992	0.18	x	50	=	9
1993	0.22	x	45	=	10
1994	0.29	x	31	=	9
1995	0.34	x	29	=	10
1996	0.43	x	26	=	11
1997	0.52	x	29	=	15
1998	0.71	x	42	=	30
1999	1.00	x	52	=	52
2000	1.10	x	47	=	52
2001	1.29	x	33	=	42
2002	1.56	x	24	=	38
2003	1.88	x	**15**	=	29
2004	2.26e	x	17	=	38

When to Sell

March 2000 was the time to sell Home Depot because the P/E was almost double the rate profits were expected to grow at.

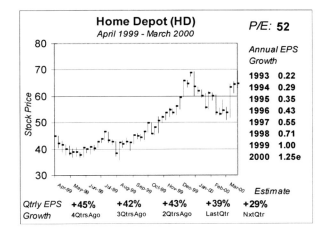

When to Buy

January 2003 was the time to buy HD back since profits grew 21% in the latest quarter and the P/E was only 13.

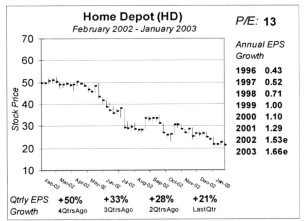

When to Hold

Holding Home Depot during this decade, and riding through the ups and downs, would have quadrupled an investor's money in 10 years.

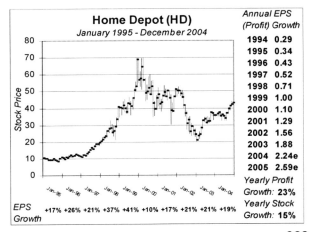

It is Obvious Stocks Were Overvalued in 2000

The stocks on the next page were large companies in 2000. When they fell from grace, they pulled the market averages down as well, just as the nifty fifty brought down the market in the 1970s. After the fall it seemed obvious these stocks were overvalued in 1999. But were they?

In *Stock for the Long Run*, Jeremy Siegel went back to the nifty fifty in 1972 to figure how overvalued those stocks were at their peaks, and found even at their highs, the nifty fifty were in fact cheap before the 1973-1974 crash:

> *What is so surprising is that many of these stocks were worth far more than even the lofty heights bid them. Investors should have paid 68.1 times the 1972 earnings for Philip Morris instead of the 24 they did pay, undervaluing the stock by almost 3-to-1. Pfizer was worth 79.5 times earnings, Merck 70.1 times and Johnson & Johnson should have sported a 74.8 multiple.*

> *In contrast to consumer brand-name stocks and pharmaceuticals, the technology stocks failed badly. IBM, which commanded a P/E ratio of 35 in the early 1970s, actually was worth only 8.9 times earnings on the basis of its future growth. It is ironic that Polaroid, the firm that sported the absolute highest P-E ratio among the original nifty fifty stocks and sold for a fantastic 94.8 times earnings in December 1972, declared bankruptcy in October 2001, and its stock price fell to 5 cents per share.*

> *Despite its mix of winners and losers, the nifty fifty stocks as a portfolio were worth almost as much as investors paid at the market peak in December 1972. An equally weighted portfolio of nifty fifty stocks was worth 39.7 times its 1972 earnings, marginally less than the 41.9 ratio that investors paid for them. Forty times earnings clearly was not too much for a good growth stock despite the conventional wisdom on Wall Street subsequent to the nifty fifty crash.[14]*

---

[14] From *Stocks for the Long Run*, Jeremy Siegel, 1994, pg 153-154, McGraw-Hill.

210

When to Sell – March 2000

Above: AIG's P/E in March of 2000 was double the quarterly profit growth rate.

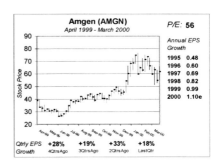

Above: Amgen's P/E of 56 was three times what AMGN's profits grew at..

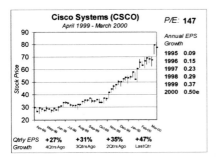

Above: Cisco's 147 P/E should have made me sell the stock, but I didn't.

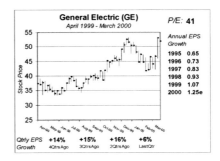

Above: GE and its 41 P/E had little upside with profit growth in the teens.

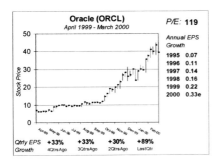

Above: The charts of Oracle and Cisco are great examples of when to sell high.

Above: Wal-Mart's P/E of 39 was high as profit growth was starting to slow.

It is Obvious Stocks are Undervalued in 2006

By 2006 stock were undervalued. As the popular Large Caps of the 1990s digested their gains after the turn of the century, the stocks were met with increased pessimism. From 2005 to mid-2006, the hot money was in commodities: oil, copper and steel because economies were expanding.

> *When investors dumped the nifty fifty, growth stocks went into a long bear market relative to value stocks. One of the reasons for this was the surge in oil stocks, which are classified as value stocks.* [15]

Between 2005 and 2006, clients were restless holding Large Cap Growth stocks. I will remember 2006 as the year I made my clients 16% annualized over the life of the relationship (double the stock market) and they left to chase something else. Consumed by the '90s, investors today are addicted to pushing for a higher return, and chase what went up last year. No way they're gonna hold a **Proctor & Gamble (PG)** for generations – the kids won't inherit it. The speculation that came in 1997 and left in 2000 was an overdose. Now, survivors are still jonesing for something better. Desperately searching for lost ground.

> *There were some remarkable parallels between...the Great Depression and during the years 1947 through the very early 1950s. Both were periods were times when it was unusually hard to obtain immediate results for clients in the face of overwhelming general pessimism. Both were times that were to prove spectacularly rewarding for those who had the patience. As I write these words in the closing weeks before the decade of the '80s is about to start, it amazes me that more attention has not been paid to restudying the few years of stock market history that started in the second half of 1946 to see whether true parallels may actually exist between that period and the present.* [16]

---

[15] From *Stocks for the Long Run*, Jeremy Siegel, 1994, pg 139, McGraw-Hill.
[16] From *Common Stocks and Uncommon Profits*, Philip A Fisher, pgs 231-232, 1996 John Wiley & Sons.

When to Buy – Nov 2006

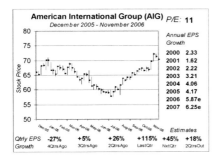

Above: AIG's P/E in the previous chart was 30. Here it's only 11.

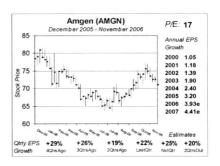

Above: The value is evident when comparing AMGN in 2000 and 2006

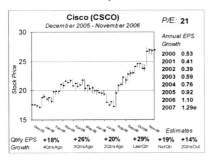

Above: CSCO and ORCL needed four years of increased profits to rebound.

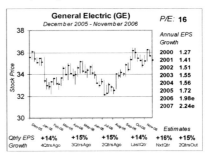

Above: GE's P/E of 16 makes the stock attractive now.

Above: CSCO and ORCL look good here but are still far from their all time highs.

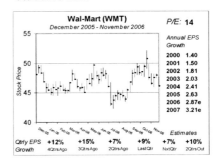

Above: Wal-Mart's rapidly-growing profits are stock market history.

As 2006 comes to a close, the great growth stocks you build a portfolio around had gone from one extreme (expensive) to another (cheap). Big solid American Growth Stocks, which were the love of investors' lives seven years earlier, now have zero downside, but no investor appeal.

Clearly, Large Cap Growth stocks have gone from ridiculously expensive to extremely cheap, which is what happens in most market cycles. These stocks have doubles or triples in their 2-3 year horizons – I just know it. Large Cap Growth has "can't lose, no miss" situations – as long as the consumer buys stocks with consistency and holds them without getting squeamish.

As in the case of other bull markets, different leaders have now emerged to lead the market. **Wal-Mart (WMT)** now struggles to post profit growth of 10% or more. New leaders include the stocks on the next page.

- **Apple (AAPL)**

- **Google (GOOG)**

- IT Outsourcers **Infosys Technology Solutions (INFY)** and **Cognizant Technology Solutions (CTSH)**

- **Akami Technologies (AKAM)**, which helps companies like MTV and Apple keep sophisticated websites online.

- **Research in Motion (RIMM)** which is about to dominate the personal phone market with its BlackBerry handheld device.

- **Genentech's (DNA)** P/E is 30, making the stock a good buy since profits are expected to grow 30% a year long term.

The stage is set for the Large Cap Growth stocks to shine once more, as they did from 1954 to 1969 and 1982 to 1999. History is repeating itself, and we're here to catch it.

What to Buy – December 2006

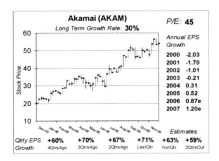

Above: AKAM helps companies like MTV and Apple keep sophisticated web sites.

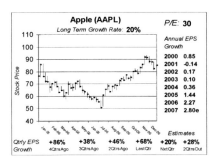

Above: I should have bought AAPL when it was in the $50s, but didn't.

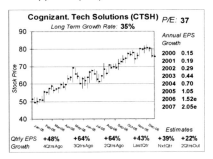

Above: Cognizant Technology Solutions is a new tech winner.

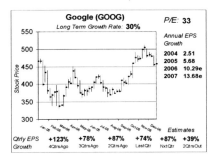

Above: Google's P/E of 33 is less than half its profit growth rate.

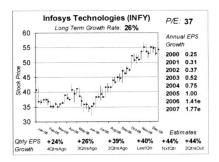

Above: INFY joins CTSH as leaders in the IT Outsourcing field.

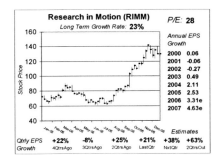

Above: RIMM is about to dominate the phone market with BlackBerry.

A Portfolio of a Successful Investor – 2006

On the opposite page is a snapshot of an account of a successful investor. This is John, a friend of mine. He likes to go against The Herd and not get suckered by the hot trend of the day.

Although many of the gains look good, you have to keep in mind the time span John had held for. Some stocks were held for years. It's nice to assume he had a good gain from the get-go, but that's not the case. Sometimes we bought and waited.

One interesting point is that the larger positions make the smaller positions look miniscule. Some of the reasoning behind the allocation is that when good stocks rise, they become a bigger portion of the portfolio. When bad stocks go down, they are consequentially a smaller percent of the whole.

Also, notice the tiny amounts put into some of the best stocks. This is because the some of the position was sold off in the past — the rest was left for the long term.

To be honest with you, there were more investors who could have been holding a portfolio such as this. But they got shook out of these stocks from the market's volatility, or had a friend who was gonna let him in on some hot real estate. Had these investors stuck with their stocks for the long run, they would have a portfolio of stocks with cost basis similar to this, maybe a little higher, or a little lower. Still, all the teaching about how to grow wealth by stock investment is virtually ignored.

In the end, finding hard stocks is easy, it's the investor himself who is greatest risk.

Shares	Company	Symbol	Open Date	Unit Cost	Mkt Price	Cost	Value	Gain/Loss	% Gain/Loss	% of Portfolio
	Value of $100,000 invested 4/03 through 12/06 (after fees)									
35	ABERCROMBIE & FITCH	ANF	11/4/2005	58	70	2021	2437	416	21%	1.23%
300	ALLSCRIPTS HEALTHCARE	MDRX			27	4692	8097	3405	73%	4.09%
L 200	ALLSCRIPTS HEALTHCARE	MDRX	3/10/2005	14						
L 100	ALLSCRIPTS HEALTHCARE	MDRX	5/3/2006	19						
50	AMERICA MOVIL	AMX	10/27/2004	14	45	722	2261	1539	213%	1.14%
100	ASTA FDG INC	ASFI	12/1/2004	23	30	2316	3044	728	31%	1.54%
50	BAIDU.COM ADR	BIDU			113	4607	5635	1028	22%	2.85%
L 30	BAIDU.COM ADR	BIDU	5/11/2006	91						
L 20	BAIDU.COM ADR	BIDU	10/30/2006	94						
100	BUFFALO WILD WINGS	BWLD			53	4570	5320	750	16%	2.69%
L 50	BUFFALO WILD WINGS	BWLD	2/9/2006	38						
L 50	BUFFALO WILD WINGS	BWLD	11/9/2006	54						
100	CAPITALSOURCE	CSE	10/16/2006	27	27	2670	2731	61	2%	1.38%
50	CAREMARK RX	CMX	4/9/2003	18	57	900	2856	1956	217%	1.44%
70	CASH AMER INTERNATIONAL	CSH	10/16/2006	41	47	2904	3283	379	13%	1.66%
100	CENTRAL EURO DIST CORP	CEDC	10/16/2006	25	30	2535	2970	435	17%	1.50%
70	CERNER CORP	CERN	4/6/2005	29	46	2029	3185	1156	57%	1.61%
100	CHINA MEDICAL TECH	CMED	11/10/2006	28	27	2811	2707	-104	-4%	1.37%
100	CITI TRENDS	CTRN			40	4377	3964	-413	-9%	2.00%
L 20	CITI TRENDS	CTRN	11/4/2005	34						
L 80	CITI TRENDS	CTRN	4/6/2006	46						
100	COACH INC	COH	7/30/2004	22	43	2170	4296	2127	98%	2.17%
100	COGNIZANT TECHNOLOGY	CTSH	9/9/2004	29	77	2892	7716	4824	167%	3.90%
150	COLDWATER CREEK INC	CWTR	8/26/2004	10	25	1436	3678	2242	156%	1.86%
50	CREDICORP	BAP	8/17/2006	35	41	1728	2047	319	18%	1.03%
50	CTRIP.COM INTERNATIONAL	CTRP	12/1/2004	27	62	1351	3119	1767	131%	1.58%
35	EXPRESS SCRIPTS INC	ESRX	4/9/2003	28	72	976	2506	1530	157%	1.27%
225	EZCORP	EZPW	9/12/2005	6	16	1424	3656	2232	157%	1.85%
50	FACTSET RESERACH SYS	FDS	10/16/2006	51	56	2556	2824	268	10%	1.43%
200	FIRST CASH FINANCIAL	FCFS	10/20/2004	12	26	2405	5174	2769	115%	2.61%
75	FOCUS MEDIA	FMCN			66	3652	4979	1327	36%	2.52%
L 50	FOCUS MEDIA	FMCN	1/9/2006	42						
L 25	FOCUS MEDIA	FMCN	4/6/2006	62						
40	GILEAD SCIENCES	GILD	11/16/2005	55	65	2192	2597	405	18%	1.31%
200	GMARKET	GMKT			24	4373	4792	419	10%	2.42%
L 100	GMARKET	GMKT	11/9/2006	21						
L 100	GMARKET	GMKT	11/16/2006	23						
100	GOL LINHAS AEREAS INTEL	GOL	11/30/2005	23	29	2293	2867	575	25%	1.45%
70	GOOGLE	GOOG			460	17,140	32,234	15,093	88%	16.28%
L 20	GOOGLE	GOOG	10/27/2004	186						
L 20	GOOGLE	GOOG	5/11/2005	231						
L 15	GOOGLE	GOOG	5/18/2005	239						
L 15	GOOGLE	GOOG	10/24/2005	348						
50	HEALTHWAYS	HWAY	4/9/2003	10	48	486	2386	1900	391%	1.21%
100	HEALTHXTRAS	HLEX	5/3/2004	14	24	1418	2410	992	70%	1.22%
60	INFOSYS TECHNOLOGIES	INFY	9/1/2004	27	55	1618	3274	1656	102%	1.65%
25	INTUITIVE SURGICAL	ISRG	10/27/2004	29	96	730	2398	1667	228%	1.21%
100	J2 GLOBAL COMM	JCOM	10/24/2005	22	27	2208	2725	518	23%	1.38%
75	JOS A BANK CLOTHIERS	JOSB	12/8/2003	15	29	1119	2201	1082	97%	1.11%
50	KOHLS	KSS	8/17/2006	62	68	3098	3422	324	10%	1.73%
50	LIFE TIME FITNESS	LTM	2/9/2006	42	49	2085	2426	341	16%	1.23%
300	NESS TECHNOLOGIES	NSTC			14	3926	4278	352	9%	2.16%
L 180	NESS TECHNOLOGIES	NSTC	5/5/2006	13						
L 120	NESS TECHNOLOGIES	NSTC	9/29/2006	13						
50	PALOMAR MED TECHS	PMTI	1/9/2006	39	51	1948	2534	586	30%	1.28%
35	PANERA BREAD	PNRA	4/6/2005	58	56	2027	1957	-70	-3%	0.99%
100	PENSON WORLDWIDE	PNSN	12/28/2006	28	27	2768	2741	-27	-1%	1.38%
50	PRICELINE.COM	PCLN	5/4/2006	29	44	1440	2181	741	51%	1.10%
100	PSYCHIATRIC SOLUTIONS	PSYS	9/8/2005	26	38	2600	3752	1152	44%	1.90%
40	RESEARCH IN MOTION	RIMM			128	4201	5111	910	22%	2.58%
L 30	RESEARCH IN MOTION	RIMM	9/29/2006	103						
L 10	RESEARCH IN MOTION	RIMM	10/10/2006	112						
100	SATYAM COMPUTER SVCS	SAY	8/2/2005	15	24	1500	2401	901	60%	1.21%
150	THE9 LTD	NCTY	3/17/2006	24	32	3666	4833	1167	32%	2.44%
50	UNITEDHEALTH GROUP	UNH	4/30/2003	30	54	1495	2687	1191	80%	1.36%
40	VARIAN MEDICAL SYSTEMS	VAR	4/9/2003	27	48	1080	1903	823	76%	0.96%
40	VIMPEL COMMUNICATIONS	VIP	9/9/2004	35	79	1394	3158	1764	127%	1.60%
50	WELLCARE HEALTH PLAN	WCG	8/15/2006	53	69	2644	3445	802	30%	1.74%
			Unrealized Gains/Losses			127,190	193,193	66,003		
			Cash				4748			
			Total Account Value				197,941			

Postscript

January 2008

After I completed this book in 2006, 2007 proved to be an excellent year for growth stocks.

In 2007, my managed portfolios increased an average of 43%. The Growth Portfolio, which closed the year with 49 stocks, gained 42%. My Aggressive Growth Portfolio, which focuses on the top ten to fifteen stocks in the Growth Portfolio, gained more than 44%. No brag, just fact.

On the opposite page are the stocks that made the most positive impact on the portfolios in 2007. But not all selections panned out. **Akamai (AKAM)** was down for the year, but now it looks better than ever. **Genentech (DNA)** was sold from the portfolio because growth slowed.

As we move into 2008, our technology companies are poised for another strong year. **Google (GOOG), Research in Motion (RIMM), Apple (AAPL)** and **Priceline.com (PCLN)** continue to fit the mold, but a recession could derail PCLN and **Focus Media (FMCN),** because spending could slow in the travel and advertising sectors. Overall, I think 2008 will be a mirror image of 2007.

What to Hold – January 2008

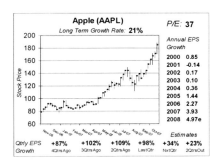

Above: *AKAM helps companies like MTV and Apple keep sophisticated web sites.*

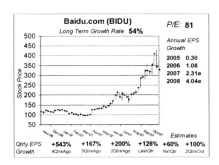

Above: *Is a good example of When to Sell High as the P/E is 81.*

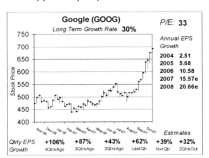

Above: *Note GOOG's made a late year run higher.*

Above: *ISRG's profit growth accelerated as it beat the street in 07.*

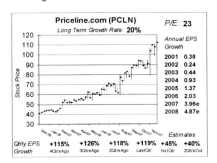

Above: *Priceline.com is still cheap at only 23 times earnings.*

Above: *Note RIMM based, then broke out at $50 – then doubled.*

A Portfolio of a Successful Investor – 2007

This is the portfolio shown in Chapter Z that had grown from $100,000 to $197,000. A strong market for Growth Stocks in 2007 helped push the portfolio to $277,000 by the end of the year. This portfolio gained 40% in 2007, and the annualized (return since inception) stood at 24%.

Factors of the Portfolio's Superb Performance

1. **This was a buy-and-hold strategy.** Note that many positions here have been held for many years. The investor, John, held for the long term, believed in the system, and didn't get shaken out by volatile stock moves.

2. **We kissed a lot of ugly frogs.** Surprisingly, only 27 of 49 from our 2006 positions made it through the following year. I guess you could say "buy and hold, if it's good enough to hold."

3. **We traded very little.** Trading is overrated. I felt that if I sold the good stocks, t hey would leave me behind.

4. **When a stock was good, we bought more.** Note five of the six the Hot Stocks of 2007 on the previous page had multiple purchases. Not all stocks are created equal, and the stocks with the best potential had higher weightings in the portfolio.

Value of $100,000 invested 4/03 through 12/07 (after fees)										
Shares	Company	Symbol	Open Date	Unit Cost	Mkt Price	Cost	Value	Gain/ Lost	% Gain/Loss	% of Portfolio
25	INTUITIVE SURGICAL INC	ISRG	10/27/2004	29	323	730	8075	7345	1006%	2.91%
50	HEALTHWAYS INC	HWAY	04/09/2003	10	58	486	2922	2436	501%	1.05%
200	VIMPEL COMMUNICATIONS	VIP	09/09/2004	7	42	1394	8320	6926	497%	3.00%
70	EXPRESS SCRIPTS INC	ESRX	04/09/2003	14	73	976	5110	4134	423%	1.84%
100	CTRIP.COM INTERNATIONAL	CTRP	12/01/2004	14	57	1351	5747	4396	325%	2.07%
50	AMERICA MOVIL SERIES L	AMX	10/27/2004	14	61	722	3070	2347	325%	1.11%
25	BAIDU.COM ADR	BIDU			390	2340	9745	7405	316%	3.51%
L 5	BAIDU.COM ADR	BIDU	05/11/2006	91						
L 20	BAIDU.COM ADR	BIDU	10/30/2006	94						
83	CVS CAREMARK CORP	CVS	04/09/2003	11	40	900	3299	2399	267%	1.19%
120	JA SOLAR HOLDINGS CO ADR	JASO	05/01/2007	22	70	2694	8377	5683	211%	3.02%
35	GOOGLE INC CL A	GOOG			691	7940	24202	16262	205%	8.72%
L 5	GOOGLE INC CL A	GOOG	10/27/2004	186						
L 20	GOOGLE INC CL A	GOOG	05/11/2005	231						
L 10	GOOGLE INC CL A	GOOG	05/18/2005	239						
100	COGNIZANT TECHNOLOGY	CTSH	09/09/2004	14	34	1446	3394	1948	135%	1.22%
150	FOCUS MEDIA HOLDING ADR	FMCN		24	57	3652	8522	4869	133%	3.07%
100	FOCUS MEDIA HOLDING ADR	FMCN	01/09/2006	21						
50	FOCUS MEDIA HOLDING ADR	FMCN	04/06/2006	31						
100	CENTRAL EURO DIST CORP	CEDC	10/16/2006	25	58	2535	5808	3273	129%	2.09%
50	CREDICORP	BAP	08/17/2006	35	76	1728	3815	2087	121%	1.38%
200	SOLARFUN POWER HLD SPON	SOLF	04/16/2007	15	33	3074	6530	3456	112%	2.35%
70	CERNER CORP	CERN	04/06/2005	29	56	2029	3948	1919	95%	1.42%
40	MOBILE TELESYSTEMS -	MBT	01/23/2007	54	102	2147	4072	1925	90%	1.47%
150	PRICELINE COM INC NEW	PCLN			115	9231	17229	7998	87%	6.21%
L 50	PRICELINE COM INC NEW	PCLN	05/04/2006	29						
L 100	PRICELINE COM INC NEW	PCLN	08/22/2007	78						
100	HEALTHXTRAS INC	HLEX	05/03/2004	14	26	1418	2608	1190	84%	0.94%
200	GAMESTOP CORP CLASS A	GME			62	6925	12422	5497	79%	4.48%
L 100	GAMESTOP CORP CLASS A	GME	03/28/2007	32						
L 100	GAMESTOP CORP CLASS A	GME	05/21/2007	37						
225	EZCORP INC CL A NON VTG	EZPW	09/12/2005	6	11	1424	2540	1116	78%	0.92%
100	SATYAM COMPUTER SVCS	SAY	08/02/2005	15	27	1500	2672	1172	78%	0.96%
121	GLOBAL SOURCES LTD	GSOL	01/04/2007	15	28	1843	3415	1572	85%	1.23%
60	INFOSYS TECHNOLOGIES F	INFY	09/01/2004	27	45	1618	2722	1104	68%	0.98%
80	GILEAD SCIENCES INC	GILD	11/16/2005	27	46	2192	3681	1489	68%	1.33%
225	CANADIAN SOLAR INC	CSIQ	11/16/2007	17	28	3823	6334	2511	66%	2.28%
150	SUNTECH POWER HOLDINGS	STP		54	82	8144	12348	4204	52%	4.45%
L 75	SUNTECH POWER HOLDINGS	STP	07/11/2007	41						
L 75	SUNTECH POWER HOLDINGS	STP	11/19/2007	67						
50	GARMIN LTD	GRMN	06/11/2007	65	97	3270	4850	1580	48%	1.75%
200	RESEARCH IN MOTION LTD	RIMM			113	15392	22680	7288	47%	8.18%
L 20	RESEARCH IN MOTION LTD	RIMM	09/29/2006	34						
L 30	RESEARCH IN MOTION LTD	RIMM	10/10/2006	37						
L 90	RESEARCH IN MOTION LTD	RIMM	07/05/2007	72						
L 60	RESEARCH IN MOTION LTD	RIMM	12/24/2007	119						
40	MEDCO HEALTH SOLUTIONS	MHS	03/08/2007	69	101	2764	4056	1292	47%	1.46%
100	COACH INC	COH	07/30/2004	22	31	2170	3058	889	41%	1.10%
100	MINDRAY MEDICAL INTL LTD	MR	06/01/2007	31	43	3050	4297	1247	41%	1.55%
20	BLACKROCK INC	BLK	05/31/2007	154	217	3080	4336	1256	41%	1.56%
50	APPLE INC	AAPL			198	7545	9904	2359	31%	3.57%
L 25	APPLE INC	AAPL	07/05/2007	131						
L 25	APPLE INC	AAPL	11/23/2007	171						
50	PSYCHIATRIC SOLUTIONS	PSYS	09/08/2005	26	33	1300	1625	325	25%	0.59%
50	HOLOGIC INC	HOLX	03/08/2007	55	69	2764	3432	668	24%	1.24%
100	BUFFALO WILD WINGS INC	BWLD	02/09/2006	19	23	1885	2322	437	23%	0.84%
200	FIRST CASH FINANCIAL	FCFS	10/20/2004	12	15	2405	2936	531	22%	1.06%
50	TRINA SOLAR LTD SPON ADR	TSL	02/22/2007	44	54	2221	2690	469	21%	0.97%
125	DOLLAR FINANCIAL CORP	DLLR	03/21/2007	26	31	3193	3836	644	20%	1.38%
100	GMARKET INC ADR	GMKT	11/09/2006	21	25	2080	2490	410	20%	0.90%
50	LIFE TIME FITNESS INC	LTM	02/09/2006	42	50	2085	2484	399	19%	0.90%
50	FACTSET RESERACH SYS INC	FDS	10/16/2006	51	56	2556	2785	229	9%	1.00%
100	YINGLI GREEN ENERGY ADR	YGE	12/19/2007	36	39	3619	3870	251	7%	1.40%
100	GUESS? INC	GES	12/31/2007	38	38	3814	3789	-25	-1%	1.37%
175	CHINA SEC&SURV TECH INC	CSR	12/19/2007	22	22	3935	3822	-113	-3%	1.38%
175	OBAGI MEDICAL PRDCTS INC	OMPI	10/03/2007	21	18	3693	3208	-485	-13%	1.16%
70	CASH AMER INTERNATIONAL	CSH	10/16/2006	41	32	2904	2261	-643	-22%	0.82%
50	AKAMAI TECH INC	AKAM	03/08/2007	51	35	2525	1730	-795	-31%	0.62%
			Unrealized Gains/Losses			152,511	277,386	124,875		
			Cash				-3			
			Total Account Value				277,383			

221

Printed in the United States
147970LV00001B/1/P

9 780615 224947